The Beacon Best of 2001

Junot Díaz, g u e s t e d i t o r

The Beacon Best of 2001

great writing

by women and men

of all colors and cultures

Beacon Press

Boston

Beacon Press
25 Beacon Street
Boston, Massachusetts 02108-2892
www.beacon.org

Beacon Press books
are published under the auspices of
the Unitarian Universalist Association of Congregations.
© 2001 by Beacon Press
Introduction © 2001 by Junot Díaz
All rights reserved
Printed in the United States of America
ISSN 1525-173X
ISBN 0-8070-6239-1 (cloth)
ISBN 0-8070-6240-5 (pbk.)

This book is printed on acid-free paper that meets the uncoated paper
ANSI/NISO specifications for permanence as revised in 1992.
Text design by Julia Sedykh Design
Composition by Wilsted & Taylor Publishing Services
06 05 04 03 02 01   8 7 6 5 4 3 2 1

contents

c o n t e n t s

1.

For the last couple of years I—a former five pages a day type guy—have not been able to write with any consistency. The reasons for my "block" are numerous and not particularly relevant, but as a result I've had more time to read newspapers and watch television, more time to notice how the world is being represented by those whom we shall call for simplicity's sake the powers-that-be. I've been aware since about the Reagan administration of the gap between the world that they *swear* exists and the world that I *know* exists. What I hadn't anticipated—I guess I should have been reading more Chomsky—is how enormous that gap had become.

2.

An example. I was recently involved in an "effort" to prevent a corporation from privatizing five public schools in New York City. The organization to which I belong began to work with one school very closely; unlike the Board of Education and the Edison Corporation, we visited the school, met with the teachers, the parents, the students. What we observed at the school was typical. It was a poorly funded, overcrowded institution with no playground, few textbooks, and in need of quality teachers. We encountered classes being held in the hallway, children sharing books, and an acute shortage of chalk.

But these details are not in themselves interesting. What's interesting is that during the subsequent "coverage" of the privatization "debate" none of the papers or news programs seemed to have seen what we did. Rather than focusing on the school's material conditions or on the government structures that systematically underfund poor minority districts (you didn't think this was happening at a white school, did you?) or on the difficulty that overcrowded "inner-city" schools encounter when trying to recruit qualified faculty, the media, the pundits, the politicians, the community leaders, the Edison Corporation—everyone it seemed, but those of us in the community—started demonizing the schools instead. They characterized the schools as "failures," "the worst schools in the city," and "basket cases." The parents (who weren't exactly thrilled that someone wanted to make money off their children's misery in order to send their own kids to private school) were called "misguided" and "foolish." As for the teachers (who thought that there was something perverse about a state abdicating its responsibility to provide quality education to its citizens), they were labeled "divisive," "Machiavellian," and "obstructionist."

The Edison Corporation, on the other hand, was accorded an amazing amount of respect. Despite the fact that the company was running a hundred-million-dollar-plus debt and had yet to achieve success rates better than the public systems it had displaced, it was called an "unsullied player," "innovative," a "new solution," and many an editorial positioned it as a "savior." Like I said, it's not the distortions, the silencing, or the erasure that astonished me. It was the increase in their power and scope. It didn't used to take so much work to pick out the Real Story; it tended to seep up through the Official Story like water. But in this case, even someone like me, who had witnessed the Real Story (by which I don't mean My Story but instead the endless myriad of stories that include My Story and the Official Story and whose conflicting sums compose the Real Story) and who should have been able to spot it peeking up through the barbwire misrepresentations, was having trouble locating it. Where was it? And where by extension was the Real World it sought to describe, a world that is complicated and unsettling and tends not to correspond to any individual, nation, or corporation's vision of itself? That world, the powers-that-be seemed to be saying, does not exist. Never has.

3.

It is this gap, between the Real Story and the Official Story, that interests me. It is inside this gap that the best writers, or at least the writers that I admire most, often reside. You don't, despite what you might think, have to be a "radical" or a "revolutionary" to be a resident of the gap. You don't have to write about dictators or the slave trade or "issues." You don't even have to write about twenty-first-century earth (hello, Octavia Butler!) Simply present a vision of the world that is complex, multi-vocal, and contradictory, that does not seek to simplify, that does not succumb to what Bruce Lee called "fearful formulas," and you will find yourself with a new address, no questions asked. All the writers gathered in this anthology have, in their own way, made a home of the gap.

4.

Patrick Rosal's "Following My Year-Long Absence" is a poem underpinned by silences that reveal more than they hide, trapdoors through which your heart might fall. And Cornelius Eady, a writer whose work I've long admired and whose intelligence and humanity I seek to emulate, evokes in "How to Do" an entire family—no, an entire community—adrift in circumstances we do not write about enough, and "Beholden to nobodies luck/ But our own." If you have been away too long from the Real World you will be jarred by writers like Felicia Ward and Reetika Vazirani ("I became those who bent me"), shattered by the likes of Dagoberto Gilb and Rhina Espaillat (whose title, "You Call Me by Old Names," is a heartbreak in itself), reborn in the word-fires of Josefina Báez (who lays bare the fate of our ciguapa myths), and made to feel awe (the tremors produced by Tim Winton's "Aquifer" and by John Frazier's "Interglacial" I still feel, beneath my shirt, my skin; Mr. Frazier in particular has dominion over silences; he too can make them speak). Herein are found titans—Chang-rae Lee and Louise Erdrich—and the fiercest of the young talents—Angela Shaw (one of the finest poets on any coast, of any color) and Maile Chapman (whose Gothic tales are without peer in their suggestiveness and their power).

Within you'll also find one of the finest "undiscovered" writers working in the United States: T. E. Holt. No book of his has ever been published and to discover him you have either to have been taught by him at Rutgers University (as I was) or have searched the stacks of your library for his work (as I did). He is a dream of Melville and Borges and Poe made flesh. His story "'Ο Λογος" is a chilling account of a deadly "communicative" illness whose first symptom is the appearance of a mysterious word upon the skin; the simple act of reading the word is all it takes to spread the plague.

I could go on—Zadie Smith's uncanny narrative legerdemain; Elissa Wald's powerfully written "descent" into stripping and into her own worrying predilections; Francisco Goldman's inspired praise-song to Mexico City; Edwidge Danticat's hurricane talent—but that would detract further from the joy of discovery.

5.

During the last week of the anti-privatization campaign, when Edison and the Board of Education and the media and the politicians were turning up the heat, I would occasionally feel myself losing heart. (There's only so much exposure to the Official Story one can take before it starts to wear on you.) I was very fortunate, however, for it was at this same time that I was reading these stories, these essays, these poems. While those of us against privatization were being knocked about in newspapers and on the news, while we were being erased and distorted into cartoons, I was sifting through journals, printing pages out from e-mail, thumbing through blurred photocopies. Would you think me sentimental if I said that the freshness and originality and humanity of these writers and their work renewed me? When billions and billions of dollars are spent trying to convince you to see the world in one particular way, isn't it something like salvation when you discover voices, brave and unwavering, who invite you to see it in another way?

6.

I leave you with Rushdie, from "Notes on Writing and the Nation": "History has become debatable. In the aftermath of Empire, in the age of superpower, under the 'footprint' of partisan simplifications beamed down to us from satellite, we can no longer easily agree on what is the case, let alone what it might mean. Literature steps into this ring. Historians, media moguls, politicians do not care for the intruder, but the intruder is a stubborn sort. In this ambiguous atmosphere, upon this trampled earth, in these muddy waters, there is work for him (her) to do."

Say word.

J u n o t D í a z

The Beacon Best of 2001

A n g e l a   S h a w

After Sleep the Wild Morning

From *Poetry*

glory's uninterrupted vine
describes a furtive turning on barbed

wire—the tendril tightening
like a python on its prey, disclosing

over and over the startled 'oh' in *ownership.*
All night my body

held its tentative
place like a marker in the latest bedside

novel. Now I take up my life mid-
sentence—wending

syntax, drifting ellipses, the irresistible
punctuation of a sometime

lover. Nothing keeps. After sleep
I savor the morning's sweet

evictions: a disturbance
of warblers: silence conquered by

birdsong, birdsong
the eloquent pause wherein silence

takes its breath. After sleep this antique
question: how long can one live

within the body like a stale guest
room, stock-still, neat as a pin, and un-

frequented? In diffuse light, only
what is most profane, only what is holy

slowly opens: the long body
of work, the mouth

of the flower—song-valve—the latent
chamber closed to those I fear

would name me.
The embrace of the bindweed—

though graceless, some say—
speaks counterclockwise

volumes: *after sleep revise*
the wild morning, take to the necessary

hedges, the precious
wayside, take

hurtful possession of your vicious twisting
vine. Stumbling into thirty,

Angela Shaw

I become my own
prey, an utterance doubling

back on itself, entwined with the furtive
turning of the past. After sleep

the leaving road contrives
to keep me

slippery, drifting, ill-
defined. The convolvulus

dilates and acquires.
I live from myself like a suitcase.

Tim Winton

Aquifer

From *Granta*

One evening not long ago I stirred from a television stupor at the sound
of a familiar street name and saw a police forensic team in waders carry
bones from the edge of a lake. Four femurs and a skull, to be precise. The
view widened and I saw a shabby clique of melaleucas and knew exactly
where it was that this macabre discovery had taken place. Through the
open window I smelt dead lupin and for a long time forgot my age. Life
moves on, people say, but I doubt that. Moves in, more like it.

Cast adrift again from middle age, I lay awake all night and travelled
in loops and ellipses while an old song from school rang in my head.

> *I love her far horizons,*
> *I love her jewelled sea,*
> *Her beauty and her terror,*
> *The wide brown land for me.*

Before dawn and without explanation, I rose, made myself coffee and began the long drive back to where I come from.

The battlers' blocks, that's what they called the meagre grid of limestone streets of my childhood. Suburban lots scoured from bush land for

an outpost of progress so that emigrants from Holland, England and the Balkans and freckly types like us, barely a generation off the farm, could participate in the Antipodean prize of home ownership. Our street wound down a long gully that gave on to a swamp. A few fences away the grey haze of banksia scrub and tuart trees resumed with its hiss of cicadas and crow song. Houses were of three basic designs and randomly jumbled along the way to lend an air of natural progression rather than reveal the entire suburb's origins in the smoky, fly-buzzing office of some bored government architect. But our houses were new; no one had ever lived in them before. They were as fresh as we imagined the country itself to be.

As they moved in people planted buffalo grass and roses and put in rubber trees which brought havoc to the septics a decade later. From high on the ridge the city could be seen forming itself into a spearhead. It was coming our way and it travelled inexorably but honestly in straight lines. The bush rolled and twisted like an unmade bed. It was, in the beginning, only a fence away.

The men of our street went to work and left the driveways empty. They came home from the city tired, often silent. They scattered blood and bone on their garden beds and retired to their sheds. All day the women of the street cleaned and cooked and moved sprinklers around the garden to keep things alive. Late in the morning the baker arrived in his van, red-cheeked from civilization, and after him the man with the veggie truck. At the sound of their bells kids spilled out into the dusty street and their mothers emerged in housecoats and pedal pushers with rollers in their hair. Everyone was working class, even the Aborigines around the corner whose name was Jones, though it seemed that these were Joneses who didn't need much keeping up with. We were new. It was all new.

At night when I was a baby my parents went walking to get me to sleep and while they were out they foraged for building materials in the streets beyond where raw sandy lots lay pegged out between brickies' sheds and piles of rough-sawn jarrah.

The old man built a retaining wall from bricks he loaded into the pram that first summer. A lot of sheds went up quickly in our street. All those jarrah planks, all that asbestos sheeting, those bags of Portland cement. It was all taxpayers' property anyway. Great evening strollers, the locals.

I grew up in a boxy double brick house with roses and a letter box, like anyone else. My parents were always struggling to get me inside something, into shirts and shoes, inside the fence, the neighbourhood, the house, out of the sun or the rain, out of the world itself it often seemed to me. I climbed the jacaranda and played with the kids across the street and came in ghosted with limestone dust. I sat on the fence and stared at the noisy blue bush and in time I was allowed to roam there.

When the road crew arrived and the lumpy limestone was tarred the street seemed subdued. The easterly wind was no longer chalky. In July and August when it finally rained the water ran down the hill towards the reedy recess of the swamp. Down the way a little from our place, outside the Dutchies' house with its window full of ornaments, a broad puddle formed and drew small children to its ochre sheen. The swamp was where we wanted to be, down there where the melaleucas seemed to stumble and the ducks skated, but our parents forbade it; they talked of quicksand and tiger snakes, wild roots and submerged logs and we made do with the winter puddle outside the van Gelders'. I remember my mother standing exasperated in the rain with the brolly over her head at dusk while I frog-kicked around in my speedos.

Eventually the road crew returned to put a drain in and my puddle became less impressive. Then a red telephone box appeared beside it. I suppose I was five or six when I learned to go in and stand on tiptoe to reach up and dial 1194 to hear a man with a BBC voice announce the exact time. I did that for years, alone and in company, listening to the authority in the man's voice. He sounded like he knew what he was on about, that at the stroke it would indeed be the time he said it was. It was a delicious thing to know, that at any moment of the day, when adults weren't about, you could dial yourself something worth knowing, something irrefutable, and not need to pay.

When I was old enough I walked to school with the ragged column that worked its way up the hill for the mile or so it took. From high ground you could see the city and the real suburbs in the distance. You could even smell the sea. In the afternoons the blue bush plain was hazy with smoke and the dust churned up by bulldozers. On winter nights great bonfires of trees scraped into windrows flickered in the sky above the yard. Beyond the splintery fence cicadas and birds whirred. Now and then the hard laughter of ducks washed up the street; they sounded like mechanical clowns in a sideshow. When summer came and the windows lay open all night the noise of frogs and crickets and mosquitoes pressed in as though the swamp had swelled in the dark.

The smallest of us talked about the swamp. Down at the turnaround where the lupins took over, we climbed the peppermint to look out across that wild expanse, but for the longest time we didn't dare go further.

Bruno the Yugo went to the swamp. He had a flat head and he was twelve. He ranged down through the reeds until dark, even though his oldies flogged him for it. Across from Bruno lived the Mannerings. They were Poms with moany Midlands accents. I could never tell when they were happy. Their house smelt of fag smoke and kero and they didn't like open windows. George the father had very long feet. He wore socks and plastic sandals. His son Alan waited for me after school some days to walk behind me and nudge me wordlessly with a knuckle for the full mile. He was twelve and scared of Bruno the Yugo. I never knew why he picked me from all the kids in our street. He never said a thing, just poked and prodded and shoved until we came down the hill to within sight of our homes. He was tall and fair, Alan Mannering, and though I dreaded him I don't think I ever hated him. When he spoke to someone else beyond me his voice was soft and full of menace, his accent broadly local as my own. Some days he threw his schoolbag up on to the veranda of his place and headed on down to the swamp without even stopping in and I watched him go in relief and envy. Mostly I played with the Box kids across the road. There were seven or eight of them. They were Catholics and most of them wet the bed though it was hard to say which ones because they all had the same ammonia and milk smell. I liked them, though they fought and cried a lot. We slipped through the bush together where there were no straight lines. Beyond the fence there were snarls and matted tangles. We hid behind grass trees and twisted logs and gathered burrs in our shirts and seeds in our hair. Eventually the Boxes began to slip off to the swamp. I always pulled up short, though, and went back to dial 1194 for reassurance.

Another Pom moved in next door. I saw him digging and stood to watch, my shadow the only greeting. I watched him dig until only his balding head showed. He winked and pointed down until I shuffled over to the lip and saw the damp earth beneath my sandals.

'The water table,' he said in a chirpy accent, 'it's high here, see. Half these fence posts are in it, you know.'

The rank, dark stink of blood and bone rose up from his side of the fence. I climbed back over the fence doubtfully.

'Looks dry this country, it does, but underground there's water. Caves of it. Drilling, that's what this country needs.'

I went indoors.

Someone hung a snake from our jacaranda out front. It was a dugite, headless and oozing. My mother went spare.

Across the road one night, Mr Box left his kids asleep in the Holden and went indoors with his wife. It was for a moment's peace, my oldies said but a moment was all they had. The station wagon rolled across the road, bulldozed the letter box and mowed down our roses.

George Mannering with the long feet mowed his buffalo grass every week with a push mower. He liked grass; it was the one thing he'd not had in England though he reminded us that English grass was finer. My mother rolled her eyes. George Mannering bought a Victa power mower and I stood out front to watch his first cut. I was there when two-year-old Charlie lurched up between his father's legs and lost some toes in a bright pink blur. All the way back inside to my room I heard his voice above the whine of the two-stroke which sputtered alone out there until the ambulance came.

I forget how old I was when I gave in and went to the swamp. It felt bad to be cheating on my parents but the wild beyond the fences and the lawns and sprinklers was too much for me. By this time I was beginning to have second thoughts about the 1194 man. My parents bought a kitchen clock which seemed to cheat with time. A minute was longer some days than others. An hour beyond the fence travelled differently across your skin compared with an hour of television. I felt time turn off.

Tim Winton

Time wasn't straight and neither was the man with the BBC voice. I discovered that you could say anything you liked to him, shocking things you'd only say to prove a point, and the man never said a thing except declare the plodding time. I surrendered to the swamp without warning. Every wrinkle, every hollow in the landscape led to the hissing maze down there. It was December, I remember. I got off my bike and stepped down into dried lupin like a man striding through a crowd. Seed pods rattled behind me. A black swan rose from the water. I went on until the ground hardened with moisture and then went spongy with saturation. Scaly paperbarks keeled away in trains of black shadow. Reeds bristled like venetian blinds in the breeze. Black water bled from the ground with a linoleum gleam.

From the water's edge you couldn't even see our street. The crowns of tuart trees were all I saw those early years before jacarandas, flame trees, and cape lilacs found their way to water and rose from yards like flags. I found eggs in the reeds, skinks in a fallen log, a bluetongue lizard jawing at me with its hard scales shining amidst the sighing wild oats. I sat in the hot shade of a melaleuca in a daze.

After that I went back alone or in the company of the Box kids or even Bruno. We dug hideouts and lit fires, came upon snakes real and imagined. I trekked to the swamp's farthest limits where the market gardens began. Italian men in ragged hats worked on sprinklers, lifted melons, turned the black earth. Water rose in rainbows across their land. I went home before dark amazed that my parents still believed me when I swore solemnly that I hadn't been down the swamp.

At school I learned about the wide brown land, the dry country. Summer after summer we recited the imperatives of water conservation. Sprinklers were banned in daylight hours and our parents watered glumly by hand.

One summer my mother announced that she'd come upon some Cape Coloureds at the nearest market garden. I thought she meant poultry of some kind. I met them on my own one day and was confused by their accents. We threw a ball for a while, two girls and me. Their skin had a mildness about it. They didn't seem as angry as the Joneses. The Joneses were dark and loud. Even their laughter seemed angry. I never had much to do with any of them. I rode past their house careful not to provoke them. They gave my little brother a hiding once. I never knew why. His nose swelled like a turnip and he nursed this grievance for the rest of his life. It made his mind up about them, he said. I kept clear. I already had Alan Mannering to worry about.

The Joneses never went near the swamp. I heard they were frightened of the dark. Their dad worked in a mine. Bruno said vile things to them and bolted into the swamp for sanctuary. It was his favourite game the year Americans went to the moon.

One sunny winter day I sat in a hummock of soft weeds to stare at the tadpoles I had in my coffee jar. Billy Box said we all begin as tadpoles, that the Pope didn't want us to waste even one of them. I fell asleep pondering this queer assertion and when I woke Alan Mannering stood over me, his face without expression. I said nothing. He looked around for a moment before pulling his dick out of his shorts and pissing over me. He didn't wet me; he pissed around me in a huge circle. I saw sunlight in his pale stream and lay still lest I disturb his aim. When he was finished he reeled himself back into his shorts and walked off. I emptied my tadpoles back into the lake.

What did he want? What did he ever want from me?

I was ten when people started dumping cars down the swamp. Wrecks would just appear, driven in the back way from behind the market gardens, stripped or burned, left near the water on soft ground where the dirt tracks gave out.

Alan Mannering was the first to hack the roof off a car and use it upturned as a canoe. That's what kids said, though Bruno claimed it was his own idea.

I was with half a dozen Box kids when I saw Alan and Bruno out on the lake a hundred yards apart sculling along with fence pickets. Those Box kids crowded against me, straining, big and small, to see. I can still remember the smell of them pressed in like that, their scent of warm milk and wet sheets. The two bigger boys drifted in silhouette out on the ruffled water. One of the Boxes went back for their old man's axe and we went to work on the scorched remains of an old F. J. Holden with nasty green upholstery. One of them came upon a used condom. The entire Box posse was horrified. I had no idea what it was and figured (correctly as it turned out) that you needed to be a Catholic to understand. Before dark

10   Tim Winton

we had our roof on the water. We kept close to shore and quickly discovered that two passengers was all it took. Some Boxes went home wet. I suppose nobody noticed.

Next day was Saturday. I got down to the swamp early in order to have the raft to myself for a while and had only pulled it from its nest of reeds when Alan Mannering appeared beside me. He never said a word. I actually cannot remember that boy ever uttering a word meant for me, but I don't trust myself on this. He lived over the road for ten years. He all but walked me home from school for five of those, poking me from behind, sometimes peppering my calves with gravel. I was in his house once, I remember the airless indoor smell. But he never spoke to me at any time.

Alan Mannering lifted the jarrah picket he'd ripped from someone's fence and pressed the point of it into my chest. I tried to bat it away but he managed to twist it into my shirt and catch the flesh beneath so that I yielded a few steps. He stepped toward me casually, his downy legs graceful.

'You're shit,' I said, surprising myself.

Alan Mannering smiled. I saw cavities in his teeth and a hot rush of gratitude burned my cheeks, my fingertips. Somehow the glimpse of his teeth made it bearable to see him drag our F. J. Holden roof to the water and pole out into the shimmering distance without even a growl of triumph, let alone a word. I lifted my T-shirt to inspect the little graze on my chest and when I looked up again he was in trouble.

When he went down, sliding sideways like a banking aircraft out there in the ruffled shimmer of the swamp's eye, I really didn't think that my smug feeling, my satisfied pity about his English teeth had caused the capsize. He didn't come up. I never even hated him, though I'd never called anyone shit before or since. After the water settled back and shook itself smooth again like hung washing, there wasn't a movement. No sign.

I went home and said nothing.

Police dragged the swamp, found the car roof but no body. Across the road the Mannerings' lawn grew long and cries louder than any mower drifted over day and night.

That Christmas we drove the Falcon across the Nullabor Plain to visit the Eastern States which is what we still call the remainder of Australia. The old man sealed the doors with masking tape and the four of us sat for days breathing white dust. The limestone road was marked only with blown tyres and blown roos. Near the border we stopped at the great blowhole that runs all the way to the distant sea. Its rising gorge made me queasy. I thought of things sucked in, of all that surging, sucking water beneath the crust of the wide brown land.

Back home, though they did not find his body, I knew that Alan Mannering was in the swamp. I thought of him silent, fair, awful, encased in the black cake mix of sediment down there.

The next year, come winter, the night air was musky with smoke and sparks hung in the sky like eyes. Bulldozers towing great chains and steel balls mowed down tuart trees and banksias.

I learned to spell aquifer.

Three doors up, Wally Burniston came home drunk night after night. His wife Beryl locked him out and if he couldn't smash his way in he lay bawling on the veranda until he passed out. Some school mornings I passed his place and saw him lying there beside the delivered milk, his greasy rocker's haircut awry, his mouth open, shoes gone.

New streets appeared even while the bush burned. I listened to the man from 1194 in the phone box that stank of cigarettes and knew that he was making the time up as he went along.

I saw the rainbow mist of the market-garden sprinklers and felt uneasy. I thought of Alan Mannering in that mist. He'd have been liquid long ago. I was eleven now, I knew this sort of thing.

As our neighbourhood became a suburb, and the bush was heaved back even further on itself, there was talk of using the swamp for landfill, making it a dump so that in time it could be reclaimed. But the market gardeners were furious. Their water came from the swamp, after all. Water was no longer cheap.

The van Gelders divorced. Wally Burniston was taken somewhere, I never found out where. One Sunday afternoon I found myself in the van Gelders' backyard scrounging for a companion when I came upon Mrs van Gelder at the back step. She had kohl around her eyes and a haircut that made her look like Cleopatra as played by Elizabeth Taylor and her short dress showed legs all the way up to her dark panties. She raised her

Tim Winton

chin at me, tapped ash from her cigarette, narrowed her eyes against the smoke that rose from her lips. I coasted near her on my bike preparing half-heartedly to ask where her son might be but she smiled and stopped me asking. From where I sat on my old chopper I saw the alarming shadow between her breasts and her smile broadened. Half her buttons were undone. She seemed sleepy. I stood against the pedals, preparing to take off, when she reached down and pulled out a breast. Its nipple was startling brown and it wore a green vein down its fuselage like a fuel line. I popped an involuntary wheelstand as I hurtled back out into the street. The slipstream of a car tugged at my shirt and tyres bawled on the fresh bitumen as someone braked and stalled. A woman began to cry. People came into the street. I swooped through them and coasted down our driveway, trembling, and hid in the shed. Months later I woke from a dream in which Mrs van Gelder leaned before me so that her cleavage showed and I stared but did not touch as dark water slurped against the plump banks of her flesh. I sat up in bed wet as a Catholic.

From one summer to the next water restrictions grew more drastic and people in our neighbourhood began to sink bores to get free unlimited groundwater. The Englishman next door was the first and then everyone drilled and I thought of Alan Mannering raining silently down upon the lawns of our street. I thought of him in lettuce and tomatoes, on our roses. Like blood and bone. I considered him bearing mosquito larvae—even being in mosquito larvae. I thought of him in frogs' blood, and of tadpoles toiling through the muddy depths of Alan Mannering. On autumn evenings I sat outside for barbecues and felt the dew settle unsettlingly. At night I woke in a sweat and turned on the bedside light to examine the moisture on my palm where I wiped my brow. My neighbour had gotten into everything; he was artesian.

At the age of twelve I contemplated the others who might have drowned in our swamp. Explorers, maybe. Car thieves who drove too close to the edge. Even, startlingly, people like the Joneses before they became working class like us. The more I let myself think about it the less new everything seemed. The houses weren't old but the remnants of the bush, the swamp itself, that was another thing altogether. Sometimes the land beyond the straight lines seemed not merely shabby but grizzled. I imagined a hundred years, then a thousand and a million. I surveyed the zeroes of a million. Birds, fish, animals, plants were drowned in our swamp. On every zero I drew a squiggly tadpole tail and shuddered. All those creatures living and dying, born to be reclaimed, all sinking back into the earth to rise again and again: evaporated, precipitated, percolated. Every time a mosquito bit I thought involuntarily of some queasy transaction with fair, silent, awful Alan Mannering. If I'm honest about it, I think I still do even now.

I knew even at ten that I hadn't willed him to die, good teeth or bad. I pulled down my T-shirt and saw him slip sideways and go without a sound, without a word. I faced the idea that he did it deliberately to spite me but he looked neither casual nor determined as he slipped into the dark. It was unexpected.

The brown land, I figured, wasn't just wide but deep too. All that dust on the surface, the powder of ash and bones, bark and skin. Out west here when the easterly blows the air sometimes turns pink with the flying dirt of the deserts, pink and corporeal. And beneath the crust, rising and falling with the tide, the soup, the juice of things filters down strong and pure and mobile as time itself finding its own level. I chewed on these things in classroom daydreams until the idea was no longer terrifying all of the time. In fact at moments it was strangely comforting. All the dead alive in the land, all the lost banking, mounting in layers of silt and humus, all the creatures and plants making thermoclines in water lit and unlit. I wasn't responsible for their coming and going either but I felt them in the water. I have, boy and man, felt the dead in my very water.

Not long after my thirteenth birthday we left the neighbourhood. We sold the house to a man who eventually married and then divorced Mrs van Gelder. News of the street trickled back to me over the years. I met people in malls, airports, waiting rooms. The man next door murdered his wife. Up the road, near the ridge, a man invented the orbital engine and the Americans tried to ruin him. Bruno went back to Serbia to burn Albanians out of their homes; someone saw him on television. One of the Box kids became a famous surgeon. Girls got pregnant. Families began to buy second cars and electrical appliances that stood like trophies on Formica shelves. The suburb straightened the bush out.

Years went by. So they say. For the past five the state has endured a historic drought. The metropolitan dams look like rock pools at ebb tide and it has long been forbidden to wash a car with a running hose. Unless they have sunk bores people's gardens have crisped and died. With all that pumping the water table has sunk and artesian water has begun to stink and leave gory stains on fences and walls. And our old swamp is all but dry. I saw it on the news because of the bones that have been revealed in the newly exposed mud. All around the swamp the ground is hardening in folds and wrinkles. The mud is veinous and cracks open to the sun.

From the moment I arrived in my air-conditioned Korean car I began to feel sheepish. Police were pulling down their tape barriers and a few news trucks wheeled away. The action was over. I sat behind the little steering wheel feeling the grit of fatigue in my eyes. I didn't even get out. What had I been expecting to see, more bones, *the* bones perhaps, have them handed over for my close inspection? Would that suddenly make me sanguine about Alan Mannering?

The swamp has a cycleway around it now and even a bird hide. Around the perimeter, where the wild oats are slashed, signs bristle with civic exhortations. Behind the pine log barriers the straight lines give way to the scruffiness of natural Australia. The sun drove in through the windscreen and the dash began to cook and give off a chemical smell. Down at the swamp's receding edge the scrofulous melaleucas looked fat and solid as though they'd see off another five years of drought. I pulled away and drove up our old street running a few laps of the neighbourhood in low gear. I took in the gardens whose European ornamentals were blanching. Only a few people were about, women and children I didn't recognize. They stood before bloody mineral stains on parapet walls with a kind of stunned look that I wondered about. A man with rounded shoulders stood in front of my old house. The jacaranda was gone. Somebody had paved where it stood to make room for a hulking great fibreglass boat. No one looked my way more than a moment and part of me, some reptilian piece of me, was disappointed that no one looked up, saw right through the tinted glass and recognized me as the kid who was with Alan Mannering the day he drowned down there on the swamp. It's as though I craved discovery, even accusation. There he is! He was there! No one said it when it happened and nobody mentioned it since. People were always oddly incurious about him. He was gone, time, as they say, moves on. They all went on without him while he rose and fell, came and went regardless. And they had no idea.

It's kind of plush-looking, the old neighbourhood, despite the drought: houses remodelled, exotic trees grown against second-storey extensions. Middle class, I suppose, which is a shock until you remember that everyone's middle class in this country now. Except for the unemployed and the dead. The city has swept past our old outpost. The bush has peeled back like the sea before Moses. Progress has made straight the way until terracotta roofs shimmer as far as the eye can see.

As I left I noticed furniture on the sandy roadside verge around the corner. Some black kids hauled things across the yard in Woolworths bags under the frank and hostile gaze of neighbours either side. An Aboriginal woman raised her fist at a man with a mobile phone and clipboard. I pulled over a moment, transfixed. Another man with a mobile phone and aviator glasses came over and asked me to move on. They were expecting a truck, he said; I complied obedient as ever, but as I gathered speed and found the freeway entry I thought of the Joneses being evicted like that. I was right to doubt the 1194 man on the telephone. Time doesn't click on and on at the stroke. It comes and goes in waves and folds like water; it flutters and sifts like dust, rises, billows, falls back on itself. When a wave breaks the water is not moving. The swell has travelled great distances but only the energy is moving, not the water. Perhaps time moves through us and not us through it. Seeing the Joneses out on the street, the only people I recognized from the old days, only confirmed what I've thought since Alan Mannering circled me as his own, pointed me out with his jagged paling and left, that the past is in us, and not behind us. Things are never over.

Tim Winton

The Lover

New Delhi, 1965

From *Callaloo*

Odd this hotel privacy. Married
and living as I did in North Carolina—
   dorm girl in her dorm room.
I took the train from Patiala,
left the girls with Ayah, and lied,
I'm with Faye and Daisy.
   Had to say what he'd approve of.
Go then, Kiran said, crushing large rupees in my hand.

Have I been here a week?
I've slept so long I can't remember for example
who was with me last night alone in bed.
Who was that figure leaning against the door?
Did he leave me this gold bangle?
I can feel its heft around my wrist;
the intricate pattern of knobs and crests,
a design from the high Mogul period of Aurangazeb.
   Who will believe me?
      *

I have come to our capitol, Delhi,
to remember our ancient past—so much and so little, a gold bangle,
    what else can I tell you?
When it slid over my hand,
I opened myself like a book is open and you hear its private pulsing.
In the quiet he said, Put your hand here
    like a bookmark to save your place.
I put my hand on my heart, and he pressed it.
He sat with me a minute, and he went away,
left something like knowledge to hinge me in the wind of myself,
to calm my legs when they shook up my precaution,
    the Asiatic kind I'm deep in.
Empire is a large land and I can't touch it.
A smile is a root my mother said don't bother.
I am dark. I am small. I married a dark talent
from a small world. This is my parcel.
The dark parent who.
The British voices who.
I became those who bent me.
I am dark. I am small.
Until he asked me to drop my shawl
and slid his finger on my shoulder,
let me taste our leisure.
It required my defiance of the small world.
He asked would you, and I said I would.
I read him. I drank up my history and peeled back the glossy lies.
I had harped on former grandeur,
but the Taj Mahal and Rome are a fantasy.
What's left is my darkness. I had found it dreadful.
He spoke to me simply of skin and I touched it.

For so many years I kept my mantra:
they are great and I am small.
I disowned myself as some have disowned me by departing.
I've slept. I've tasted my own milk.
I am dark. I slept in darkness.

Reetika Vazirani

I feel a circle on my wrist, it's surplus of hours,
more today, more tomorrow.
I'll raise my girls, then I'll be back.
I've tasted the drink and crave these minutes.
If I never sip this again I already tasted the morning.

Water Child

From *The New Yorker*

The letter came on the first of the month, as usual. It was written, as most of them were, in near-calligraphic style, in indigo-blue ink, on see-through airmail paper.

> *Ma Chère Nadine,*
> *We are so happy to have this occasion to put pen to paper to write to you. How are you? All is well with us, grace à Dieu, except your father, whose health is, as always, unreliable. Today it is his knees. Tomorrow it will be something else. You know how it is when you are old. He and I both thank you for the money you sent last month. We know it is difficult for you, but we are grateful. This month your father hopes to see yet another doctor. We have not heard your voice in a while and our ears ache for it. Please call us.*

She signed it, "Your mother and father who embrace you very tightly."

Three weeks had gone by since the letter arrived, and Nadine still hadn't called. She had raided her savings to wire double the usual amount but hadn't called. Instead she took the letter out each day as she ate a tuna melt for lunch in the hospital cafeteria, where each first Friday for the last two years she had added a brownie to her meal for scheduled variety.

Every time she read the letter, she tried to find something else between the lines, a note of sympathy, commiseration, condolence. But it simply wasn't there. The more time went by, the more brittle and fragile the letter became. Each time she held the paper between her fingers she wondered how her mother had not torn it with the pen she'd used to compose each carefully inscribed word. How had the postal workers in both Port-au-Prince and Brooklyn not lacerated the thin page and envelope? And how had the letter not turned to dust while rubbing against the lining of the left pocket of her nurse's uniform during the bus ride to work? Or in her purse in her locker, in the artificial heat all day long?

She carefully folded the letter once again and replaced it in her purse as one of her colleagues approached the small corner table by the window that she occupied in solitude for a whole hour each working day. The colleague, Josette, kissed her on both cheeks while fumbling in her pocket for lunch money. As Nadine's lunch hour was winding down, Josette's was just beginning.

Nadine smiled both at Josette and to herself at this ability of Josette's to make an ordinary encounter feel so intimate, then turned her face to the view outside, to the brown buildings and their barred windows, coated with a thin sheet of early-January frost. She let her eyes linger on the nursing station of the psych ward across the alley and entertained a vision she often had of seeing a patient dive out of one of the windows. Would she leap out of her chair, run to the elevator, down to the alley separating the two buildings, or would she simply sit there and finish the last quarter glass of her skim milk?

"Ms. Hinds is back from I.C.U.," Josette was saying. "She's so *sezi* about not being able to talk that Dr. Vega had to give her a sedative."

Nadine and Josette worked both ends of Ear, Nose, and Throat and saw many post-op patients wake up bewildered to discover that their total laryngectomies meant that they would no longer be able to use their voices to communicate. No matter how the doctors and nurses prepared them, it was still a shock.

Josette always gave Nadine a report on the patients when she came to take over the table. She was one of the younger Haitian R.N.s, one of those who came to Brooklyn in early childhood and spoke English with no accent at all, but she liked to throw in a Creole word here and there in conversation to flaunt her origins. Aside from the brief lunch encounters, and times when one or the other needed a bit of extra help with a patient, they barely spoke at all.

"I am going now," Nadine said, rising from her seat. "My throne is yours."

When she returned to her one-bedroom condo in Canarsie that evening, Nadine was greeted by voices from the large television set that she kept turned on twenty-four hours a day. Along with the uneven piles of newspapers and magazines scattered between the fold-out couch and the floor-to-ceiling bookshelves in her living room, the television was her way of bringing voices into her life that required neither reaction nor response. At thirty-two, she had tried other hobbies—jogging, journal writing, drawing, Internet surfing—but these tasks had demanded either too much effort or too much superficial interaction with other people.

She took off the white sneakers that she wore at work and remained standing to watch the last few minutes of a news broadcast. It wasn't until a game show had begun that she pressed the playback button on her beeping answering machine.

Her one message was from Eric, her former beau, suitor, lover, the near father of her nearly born child.

"*Alo, allô,* hello," he stammered, creating his own odd pauses between Creole, French, and English, like the electively mute, newly arrived immigrant children whose worried parents brought them in for consultations, even though there was nothing wrong with their vocal cords.

"Haven't heard from you." He chose English. Long pause. "O.K. Bye."

Whenever he called her now, which was about once a month since their breakup, she removed the microcassette from the answering machine and placed it on the altar she had erected on top of the dresser in her bedroom. It wasn't anything too elaborate. There was a framed drawing that she had made of a cocoa-brown, dewy-eyed baby that could as easily have been a boy as a girl, the plump fleshy cheeks resembling hers and the high forehead resembling his. Next to the plain wooden frame were a dozen now dried red roses that Eric had bought her as they'd left the clinic after the procedure. She had read about a shrine to unborn children in Japan, where water was poured over little altars of stone to honor them, so she had filled her favorite drinking glass with water and a small pebble and had added that to her own shrine, along with a total of now three microcassettes with messages from Eric, messages she had never returned.

That night, the apartment seemed oddly quiet in spite of the TV voices. She took out her mother's letter for its second reading of the day, ran her fingers down the delicate page, and reached for the phone to dial her parents' number. She'd almost called many times in the last three months but had lost her nerve, thinking that her voice might betray all that she could not say. She nearly dialled the whole thing this time. There were only a few numbers left when she put the phone down, tore the letter into two, then four, then eight, then countless pieces, collapsed among her old magazines and newspapers, and wept quietly.

Another letter arrived at Nadine's house a week later. It was on the same kind of airmail paper, but this time the words were meticulously typed. The "a"s and "o"s, which had been struck over many times, created underlayers, shadows, and small holes within the vowels' perimeters.

Ma chère Nadine,

Your father and I thank you very much for the extra money. Your father used it to see a doctor, not about his knees, but his prostate that the doctor says is inflamed. Not to worry, he was given some medications and it seems as if he will be fine for a while. All the tests brought us short for the monthly expenses, but we will manage. We would like so much to talk to you. We wait every Sunday afternoon, hoping that you will return to our beautiful routine. We pray that we have not abused your generosity, but you are our only child and we only ask for what we need. You know how it is when you are old. We have tried to call you, but we are always greeted by your answering machine. In any case, we wait to hear from you.

Your mother and father who embrace you tightly.

The next day, Nadine ignored her tuna melt altogether to read the letter over many times. She did not even notice the lunch hour pass, and Josette was standing over her at the table sooner than she expected. Josette, like all the other nurses, knew not to ask any questions about Nadine's past, present, future, or her international-looking mail. Word circulated quickly from old employees to new arrivals that Nadine Marie Osnac was not a friendly woman. Anyone who had sought detailed conversations with her, or who had shown interest in sharing the table while she was sitting there, had met only with cold silence and a blank stare out to the psych ward, where the winter frost was still clinging to the window bars. Josette, however, still occasionally ventured a social invitation, since they were both from the same country and all.

"Some of the girls are going to the city after work," Josette was saying. "A little *banbòch* to celebrate Ms. Hinds' discharge tomorrow."

"No, thanks," Nadine said, departing from the table a bit more abruptly than usual.

That same afternoon, Ms. Hinds began throwing things across her small private room, one of the few in the ward. Nadine nearly took a flower vase in the face as she rushed in to help. Unlike the other patients in the ward, Ms. Hinds was a nonsmoker. She was also much younger—twenty-five years old. When Nadine arrived, Ms. Hinds was thrashing about so much that the nurses, worried that she would yank out the metal tube inserted in her neck and suffocate, were trying to pin her down to put restraints on her arms and legs. Nadine quickly joined in the struggle, assigning herself Ms. Hinds' right arm, pockmarked from months of I.V.s in hard-to-conquer veins.

"Where's Dr. Vega?" Josette shouted as she caught one of Ms. Hinds' random kicks in her chest. Nadine lost her grip on the I.V. arm. She was looking closely at Ms. Hinds' face, her eyes tightly shut beneath where her eyebrows used to be, her thinner lower lip protruding defiantly past her upper one as though she were preparing to spit long distance in a contest, her whole body hairless under the cerulean-blue hospital gown, which came with neither a bonnet nor a hat to protect her now completely bald head.

"The doctor's on his way," one of the male nurses said. He had a firm hold of Ms. Hinds' left leg could not pin it down to the bed long enough to restrain it.

"Leave her alone," Nadine finally suggested to the others.

They all looked up at her at the same time, their own exhaustion and frustration forcing them to release Ms. Hinds' extremities. One by one, they slipped a few steps back to protect themselves. With her need to struggle suddenly gone, Ms. Hinds coiled into a fetal position and sank into the middle of the bed.

"Let me be alone with her," Nadine said.

The others lingered awhile, as if not wanting to leave, but they had other patients to see to, so, one at a time, they backed out the door.

"Ms. Hinds, is there something you want to tell us?" Nadine lowered the bed rail to give Ms. Hinds a limited sense of freedom.

Ms. Hinds opened her mouth wide, trying to force air past her lips, but all that came out was the hiss of oxygen and mucus filtering through the tube in her neck.

Nadine looked over at the night table, where there should have been a pad and pen, but Ms. Hinds had knocked them over onto the floor with the flower arrangements and magazines her parents had brought for her.

Nadine walked over and picked up the pad and pen and handed them to Ms. Hinds.

"I am here, Ms. Hinds. Go ahead."

Ms. Hinds grabbed the pad eagerly, scribbled down a few quick words, then held it up for Nadine to read. At first Nadine could not understand the handwriting. It was unsteady and hurried and the words ran together, but she sounded them out, one at a time, with some encouragement from Ms. Hinds, who moved her head a few inches up and down when Nadine guessed correctly.

"I cannot speak," Nadine made out.

"That's right," Nadine said. "You cannot express yourself the way you used to."

Ms. Hinds grabbed the pad again and scribbled another sentence. "I am an elementary school teacher."

"I know," Nadine said.

"WHY ARE THEY SENDING ME HOME LIKE THIS?"

"We are sending you home," Nadine said, "because we have done all we can for you here. Now you must work with a speech therapist. You can get an artificial larynx, a voice box. There are many options. The speech therapist will help you."

It was a pep talk that Nadine hated giving to the patients, the "you will make it after all" talk.

That night at home, Nadine found herself more exhausted than usual. With a television movie as white noise, she dialled Eric's home phone number, hoping that she was finally ready to hear his voice for more than the twenty-five seconds her answering machine allowed.

His wife answered the phone, and to avoid initiating a conversation Nadine listened. She listened to the many "Hello"s of the wife and she listened to the wife's own television in the background, which was on a different channel than hers; she heard something drop, maybe a dinner plate that the wife was picking up from the family table after a meal; she listened to a young child's voice scream, "Papi, Papi, Mommy broke something." And at last she heard Eric's voice growing louder, moving closer to the phone, speaking gently to his wife in French, *"Qu'est-ce qu'il y a, chérie?"* Then she heard the transfer from the wife's breath to his, and she hoped that perhaps he would recognize her breathing on the other end of the line, but he said his own series of "Hello"s and then hung up.

She picked up the phone again to call him back to say something predictable like "It is time she knew." But maybe the wife already knew. So she decided to call her parents instead. Talking to them always made her wish for a life where children were parented even after they had married and moved into a house down the street. Ten years ago her parents had sold everything they owned, had moved from what passed for a lower-middle-class neighborhood to one on the edge of a slum, in order to send her to nursing school abroad. Ten years ago she had dreamed of seeing the world, of making her own way in it. Ten years ago she had desired her solitude more than anything. These were the intangibles that she had proposed to her mother the seamstress and her father the camion driver in the guise of a nursing career. This is what they had sacrificed everything for. But she always knew that she would repay them. And she had, with half her salary every month, and sometimes more. In return what she got was the chance to parent them rather than have them parent her. Talking to them, however, always made her wish to be the one guarded, rather than the guardian, to be reassured now and then that some wounds could heal, that some decisions would not haunt her forever.

"Manman." Her voice immediately dropped to a whisper when her mother's came over the phone line, squealing with happiness.

"Papa, it is Nadine." For every decibel Nadine's voice dropped, her mother's rose. "My love, we were so worried about you. How are you? We were so worried."

"I'm fine, Manman."

"You sound cold. You sound down. We have to start planning again when you can come or we can come see you, as soon as Papa can travel."

"How is Papa?"

"He is right here. Let me put him on. He would be very glad to speak with you."

Suddenly her father was on the phone, his tone calmer, but excited in its own way. "We were waiting so long for this call, *chérie*."

"I know, Papa. I am sorry I haven't called."

They never spoke of sad and difficult things during these phone calls, of money or illnesses or doctors' visits. Papa always downplayed his aches and pains, which her mother would detail in the letters. There was no time for anything but joy. Events were relayed briefly, a list of accomplishments, no discussion of failures or pain, which could spoil moods for days, weeks, and months, until the next phone call.

"Do you have a boyfriend?" Her mother took back the phone. Nadine could imagine her skipping around their living room like a child's ball bouncing. "Is there anyone in your life?"

"I have to go, Manman."

"So soon?"

"I work early tomorrow. I promise I will call again."

The next day, Nadine watched as Ms. Hinds packed her things and changed into a bright-yellow oversized sweatsuit and matching cap while waiting for the doctor to come and sign her discharge papers.

"My mother bought me this hideous outfit," Ms. Hinds wrote on the pad, which was now half filled with words: commands to the nurses, up dates to her parents left over from the previous afternoon's visit. Ms. Hinds climbed up on the bedside closer to the door, her bony legs dangling. She reached up and stroked the protruding tip of the metal tube in her neck.

"Is someone coming for you?" Nadine asked.

"My parents," she wrote.

"Good," Nadine said. "The doctor will be here soon."

Nadine spent half her lunch hour staring at the barred windows on the brown building across the alley, watching the psych nurses scribbling in charts and filing them, rushing to answer sudden calls from the ward. No one would ever get past the wall of nurses to reach the window and dive to the alley, she realized, unless it was a nurse with a blowtorch and a death wish.

Josette walked up to the table earlier than usual, obviously looking for her.

"What is it?" Nadine asked.

"*Se* Ms. Hinds," said Josette. "She would like to say goodbye to you."

She thought of asking Josette to tell Ms. Hinds that she could not be found, but fearing that this would create some type of conspiratorial camaraderie between them, decided against it.

Ms. Hinds and her parents were waiting by the elevator bank in the ward. Ms. Hinds was sitting in a wheelchair with her discharge papers and a white plastic bag full of odds and ends on her lap. Her father, a strapping, hulking man, was clutching the back of the wheelchair with moist, nervous hands, which gripped the chair more tightly for fear of losing hold. The mother, a plump, fleshy woman, whose height nearly matched the father's, looked as though she were fighting back cries, tears, a tempest of anger, barters with God.

Instead she fussed, trying to wrench the discharge papers and the white plastic bag from her daughter, irritating Ms. Hinds, who raised her pad from beneath the pile of papers and scribbled quickly, "Nurse Osnac, these are my parents, Carole and Justin Hinds."

Nadine shook each parent's hand in turn.

"Glad to make your acquaintance," said the father.

The mother said nothing.

"Thank you for everything," said the father. "Please share our thanks with the doctors, the other nurses, everyone."

The elevator doors suddenly opened and they found themselves staring at the bodies that filled it to capacity—the doctors and nurses travelling between floors, the walk-in patients from floors above them, the visitors. The Hindses let the doors close and the others departed without them.

Ms. Hinds turned to an empty page toward the back of her pad and wrote, "Goodbye, Nurse Osnac."

"Good luck," Nadine said.

Another elevator opened. There were fewer people in it this time, and enough room for all the Hindses and the discharge nurse. The father pushed the wheelchair, which jerked forward, nearly dumping Ms. Hinds face first into the elevator.

The elevator doors closed behind them sharply, leaving Nadine alone facing a distorted reflection of herself in the wide, shiny metal surface. She thought of her parents, of Eric, of the pebble in the water glass in her bedroom at home, all of those things belonging to the widened, unrecognizable woman staring back at her from the closed doors.

Ha Jin

The Taiping Leaders

From *Harper's*

In our godless land every hero can become a god. When Hong fails the Confucian examination again, his dream of becoming an official is shattered, and he's carried all the way from Canton back to Hua village. We gather along the walls around his home to get a look at him. Stretched out in a sedan chair, he looks as unconscious as a dead man. It's a quiet morning; even the chickens and pigs are silent. Hong's bride wails shamelessly while his stepmother says to his father that it would have been better if Hong had remained our village schoolteacher and never left home. Hong used to be a cheerful man, though sometimes he seemed dull.

For a whole month he lies in bed, delirious. Sometimes he sweats and shakes like an epileptic. Sometimes he jumps out of bed, swings an imaginary sword, and sidles around, shouting, "Kill this devil, and the one over there." His family, believing he's mad, keeps him strictly indoors.

In his sleep Hong often sees himself ascend to heaven, where he joins God's family. God is a burly man, wearing a long golden beard and a dragon robe. God and his wife treat Hong like a son and let him dine with them twice a day, though Hong stays in a marble mansion alone, attended by a group of angels. Every morning, after a hearty breakfast of honey wine and fruit, he studies under the guidance of a silver-bearded

30

seraph. Once when he cannot answer a question about human suffering, a young lady turns up from behind a pavilion and gives him a clue written on a white silk handkerchief. He recognizes her! She is Jesus' wife, whom Hong later will regard as his second mother.

What a blissful place heaven is! It's full of buxom maidens, all pure like fresh lotus flowers. Cranes, pelicans, and herons land on your shoulders without any fear. Shops, theaters, libraries, bath parlors, inns, and restaurants are open to everyone; no money is in use. Most amazing are the vast orchards, all laden with fruits—peaches as fat as pumpkins, apples like babies' faces, cherries and grapes as large as duck eggs. Wherever Hong goes, the air smells of flowers and echoes with soothing music. No one here seems to care about the passage of time.

For years after Hong returns to this filthy world, he cannot figure out the meaning of his heavenly dreams. Not until he reads a tract given him by a young American missionary does he realize he belongs to God's family—he is the youngest son, thirteen years Jesus' junior. He was sent down to replace Christ, to cleanse the earth and redeem it for their Father. He remembers God's sorrowful tears over the deluded, ungrateful human race.

Then he, his cousin, and several of us, who are his friends, go to Thistle Mountain, where we begin to pore over an abridged Bible. We find that his name, the character "Hong," is mentioned numerous times in the scriptures, so every one of us is convinced that Hong is God's son. And Hong begins to baptize people in the manner described in the tract. He travels from village to village, at times followed by crowds over two hundred strong. We are peaceful at first, but the river bandits, local militia, and government troops keep harassing us. Some of our brothers are arrested by officials, and we have to pay high ransoms to get them back. Many of them are beaten to death; some have perished in prison.

After our ranks have grown larger than twenty thousand and after we have captured Yungan, a city on the Sha River, our generals train us to become fearless soldiers, then lead us to attack the demons—the Manchu officials and their troops. Our army is invincible, sweeping away our enemy like a gust of wind tossing a tattered mat. What's more, we are well disciplined: nobody is allowed to take anything away from the civilians; looting is prohibited; all spoils belong to the public treasury; officers and soldiers are equal, as we are all brothers and sisters; men and women are kept in separate camps; sex is forbidden, even among married couples, because we are instructed that the genuine union of men and women can happen only after our final victory—the establishment of our earthly paradise. Offenders against the laws will be executed publicly. Sometimes when we arrive at a town, its citizens will gather along the roadside to welcome us.

One day, one of Hong's closest friends, Yang, who used to be a charcoal burner in our home province, suddenly falls into a trance. He's an emaciated, yellow-faced man, who used to be fond of opium, gambling, and prostitutes but gave up his bad habits all at once after he met Hong. Many of us witness his sudden transformation into the Holy Spirit. It's a windy afternoon. The sun, blurred and low, seems to have grown toothed petals like a gigantic flower. Yang collapses on the drill ground in front of four hundred men, ranting and kicking his thin legs. "I'm the Holy Ghost, I'm your Father," he raves. "All, all of you must follow my words from now on. I am the king of kings. Listen and obey . . ."

Thunderstruck, we don't know what to do. We just watch him lying on his back and shouting with his eyes closed and with foam at his mouth.

An orderly is sent to inform Hong of what's going on. Within ten minutes Hong arrives on his black steed. "Get up, Brother Yang," he pleads. "Don't make a fool of yourself like this."

We all hold our breath, fearful that he's going to have Yang flogged.

To our surprise, the glassy-eyed Yang orders Hong solemnly, "Kneel down, my son. You slapped your seventh concubine again last night, didn't you? So you sinned against me, your Father. For months you have spoiled your baby son. You have let him tear cloth just because he likes the sound of it. You have let him feed his monkeys rice and stewed pigeon while there are still beggars on the streets. Now I must teach you a lesson so you will remember that I sent you down not to enjoy happiness but to suffer for all living creatures. Get ready to accept your punishment."

"Shut up!" a young officer barks at him.

But somehow Hong is visibly shaken by Yang's voice. He looks pallid and dazed. Sweat breaks out across his brow. To our astonishment, he lifts the front end of his robe, falls on his knees, and bows his head.

"Do what he says," he tells us.

"Give him one hundred lashes!" screams the Father.

Two strapping fellows step forward and each with a bull's pizzle begin thrashing Hong, who wriggles but doesn't utter a sound. Throughout the punishment he remains on his knees and grits his teeth to suppress his moaning. He's a tough man but is so battered that he can no longer rise to his feet when the flogging is over. His bodyguards help him up and place him on his horse. Blood drips from his fingertips.

For a whole week Hong stays in bed. Afterward he appoints Yang the East King, second only to himself in power. Fortunately, Yang doesn't speak as our Holy Father very often; God visits him only a few times a year.

Meanwhile, we've never stopped fighting the Manchu troops. From time to time we have to abandon a town or a city to avoid annihilation. Hong has another bosom friend, General Hsiao, who used to be a peasant and occasionally hired himself out as a porter. Like Yang, Hsiao manages to get admitted to the divine household, and he, too, begins to have trances. He's a giant, tall and thickset, but he's smart and nimble, skilled in martial arts. We all respect him, because he always charges into battle at the front of his troops and often shares with them his meat and wine, and also because he hates foreign devils; once he singlehandedly felled a band of them. He's straightforward and speaks in a voice like a bell. Unlike Yang's godly transformation, Hsiao's is more peaceful; he merely calls Hong "my younger brother" and himself Jesus Christ.

This takes place at the end of a banquet. Hsiao, in a drunken stupor, lies among the dishes on a table and addresses us like an orator: "God, our Holy Father, sent me down to see how well you were faring. He is anxious to hear news of victory from you. He wants me to inform you that you must not attach yourself to any mountain or river. You must head toward the big city, where together with your people you can set up the Small Paradise. Do not fear the official army, which only appears powerful but is actually a paper tiger . . ."

Hong stops the band from playing "The Moon Is Rising" and drops on his knees. We all follow suit, listening to the message from heaven.

So Hong accepts General Hsiao as his elder brother Jesus Christ. He appoints him the West King and allows him to have a territory, a large band, a staff of over two hundred people, a harem of eleven women. Hong often consults Hsiao on important matters. Whenever Hsiao speaks as Jesus, his sacred words are mysterious and sometimes difficult to fathom, but almost without exception they point us in the right direction.

With the guidance of the Father and the Elder Brother, we fight one battle after another with the government troops. We are so invincible that people call us the "Heavenly Army." Within three years we take Nanking, the largest city on the Yangtze River, which Hong turns into the Celestial Capital. He increases the height of the city wall by four feet, has Buddhist temples torn down to get building materials for his palace, sets up a new calendar, and orders his subjects to call him the Sovereign, the ruler of the Heavenly Kingdom of Great Peace. Indeed, people now live peacefully under his reign. Food is plenty, since Nanking is surrounded by fertile land. For a time we all enjoy living under our own dynasty.

Then Hong dispatches two armies simultaneously on expedition. They are to go by different routes to Peking to topple the Manchu Court, the den of the demons, so that we can unify all of China.

Unfortunately, our northern expeditionary army, the stronger of the two forces, reaches only as far as Tientsin, a city almost seventy miles east of Peking, unable to march farther to stab the dark heart of the Manchu regime. Later, the official army, helped by the European and American devils, besieges our Celestial Capital. Nanking is soon filled with ruins and paupers. Famine and plague are rampant; vultures and dogs fatten up on corpses. One by one our kings and generals are wiped out by one another and by enemy troops.

Yet even long after the collapse of our dynasty, we still worship our leaders, believing they have ascended to the Kingdom of God. They left us only because they had finished their stay on earth. So we won't bring them down from heaven, their august names still invoked in thousands of our prayers.

Josefina Báez

A 1 2 3 Portrait of a Legend

From *Callaloo*

Our deity Ciguapa arrived in New York too.
The subway steps changed her nature. In the ups and down to and
    from the
silver grey fast worms, her feet became as everybody else's in the
    rush hour crowd.
She did not notice the drastic change.
This was the first sign of assimilation
—a concept not to be understood but experienced.
And Ciguapa cut her hair; maybe to be in vogue or just to simplify
her rituals.
Her lover was not a hunter as the legend goes.
He was a medical doctor by profession turned taxi driver by
    necessity.
He, the gypsy Caribbean, worked for an uptown car service: La
    Base Tuya.
In this base, our deity was codified to a mere 10-13. It meant
    mistress or wife.
We never knew and she never cared.

    *

Their love was filled with few words, passionate actions, fast merengues, tasty
sancochos and predictable trips to la remesa El Sol Sale Para Todos.
These trips energized by green dollars reforested the island.

Ciguapa works in a factory making pinkish dolls.
Dolls that she never had. Dolls dulled by the unique smell of new.
Earning less than the minimum, she managed to pay an immigration lawyer that she never met.
She got her green card.
It was not green.

Now she prepared herself to visit the Dominican Republic. What a triumph!!
She made it.
She made it! She made it?
Huge suitcases, bought at 14th Street, were filled with unthinkable, unnecessary items.
Items to be sold at laughable prices. Prices calculated in dollars, paid in pesos.
Laughable reality. She whose laugh is based on a constant and bitter cry.
Constant nostalgia. Bitter reality. Unheard cry.

Here is no man's land. Here is no woman's stand. You can become what you
are not by circumstances, opportunity, luck, unluck, karma.
You can become a saint or forget your divinity.

My telephone is being checked for trouble
the ATM machine coldly informs me
in Spanish informed me there is not enough funds
no it did not clear out yet and out-of-state check 4 working days
dispossess dispossess
premises must be vacant if money is not received before 5:00 pm

Josefina Báez

Susan B. Anthony and Kennedy coins were traded by their face
   value 1971 1973 1980
issued by law treasured spent by dawn
2 dollar bills were the personified luck
2 dollar bills were the great surprise
the educational loan people/voice activated machine got my
   address
no tokens no tokens MTA does not accept pennies
mine from this pockets shaven not from heaven
there's no black box to swallow my Dominican quarter

every letter is a bill threatening me to mess the credit that I don't
   have. My face
and my hands told the ATM line that I did not have money
hope is never transformed in dollars

he dissed me he left too as the days with extra money for pints of
   ice cream
he dissed me as the nights with $12 for 2 foreign films from the
   video-rental
I told you so I told you so filled the wire
I told you so I told you so screams my mind tired

please deposit 5 cents or your call will be terminated. This is a
   recording.
Thank you.

Agha Shahid Ali

There Is No God But

From *New England Review*

in the "Name of the Merciful" let night begin.
I must light lamps without her at every shrine?
God then is only the final assassin.

The prayers end. Emptiness waits to take her in.
With laments found lost on my lips, I resign
myself to His every Name. Let night begin

without any light, for as they carry the coffin
from the mosque to the earth, no stars shine
to reveal Him as only the final assassin.

The mourners, at the dug earth's every margin,
fill emptiness with their hands. Their eyes meet mine.
"In the Name of the Merciful" I let night begin.

In the dark the marble of each tomb grows skin.
I tear it off. I make a holocaust. I underline
God is the only, the only assassin

as flames put themselves out, at once, on her shrine
(they have arrived like moths from temples and mosques).
With no Name of His then must this night begin.

Nega Mezlekia

From "EXODUS: An Ethiopian Road Trip"

From *Transition*

The only road out of Jijiga was a narrow alley between Mt. Karamara and Mt. Chinaksen. Karamara is the tallest of three mountain peaks that surround the city. As a kid, I had looked down on Jijiga from its towering height while playing with friends. Now, we were trying to pass through the alley without being intercepted by the invading Somalis. Once we arrived behind the mountain curtain, the Ethiopian army ordered us to set up camp in the valley. They hoped to reclaim the town before long.

There were no forests in this region, only a sparse growth of acacia trees that offered little shade from the unforgiving sun. The valley is home to wandering packs of monkeys—monkeys unlike any others in the country. They are immense, combative, and stubborn, known to ram heavy boulders onto passing cars.

The city of Harar was only seventy-five miles from Jijiga, but it took us almost two weeks to get there, and those two weeks left an indelible mark. Those two weeks will be remembered in history as a time when it rained upward, a time when people shed tears that they caught on the tips of their fingers and flung at the faces of treacherous gods.

The exodus was a godsend for teenage boys who aspired to play cops and robbers. They were issued real guns with live bullets and could shoot without asking their mothers' permission. I was given an M-1 rifle, but I soon discovered it was more dangerous to me than to the enemy. It was cumbersome, it recoiled when I fired it, and it was almost as tall as me. I dumped it in a bush and walked over to a militiaman who had an extra Kalashnikov. I borrowed it, along with two clips of bullets. He reminded me to give it back before we got to Harar.

The guns were supposed to protect our families from unsavory elements in the jungle. The army did not expect civilians to fight the war for them—in fact, the old rifles were useless against the invading army, and even tanks were of no avail: the Somalis were firing long-range cannons at us, their location a mystery. Once, when Ethiopian jets bombed what was rumored to be the Somalis' secret base, the firing let up for a while. But even this did not slow them for long.

Running into wild beasts was never a concern during the exodus; they had long since decided to give us wide berth. On the day of the massacre in Jijiga, the hyenas ended diplomatic relations with us, withdrawing their missions from our towns and villages. The lions made a parable of our carpet-bombing the countryside: they taught their young that killing neighbors indiscriminately was the truest form of beastliness, too beastly even for them. The elephants regarded our movements as a threat to their lifestyle, an irresponsible squandering of natural resources; they vowed never to set eyes on us again.

During the exodus, survival depended on numbers. You needed more than one person to find food. You had to have connections to get medicine. Water was rationed; if you didn't get tipped off to the arrival of the water truck in advance, you might well spend the whole day waiting in line under the scorching heat. With more than twenty thousand refugees leaving Jijiga, the barest necessities of life were purchased by constant struggle.

I saw people lose limbs to antipersonnel mines: they survived their injuries only to become liabilities to their loved ones. On a journey where the clothes on your back felt like a burden, it was selfish to expect others to care for you. Early on, I resolved that if I ever found myself in such a predicament, Mam would not be forced to decide what to do with her son. Unbeknownst to her, I communicated my decision to a group of young men whose animal instincts I could count on.

The group that I belonged to consisted of a young officer from the infantry, also a native of Jijiga, and two boys I knew from the neighborhood back home. The four of us roamed together in the morning, indulging our boyish imaginations, pretending to be detectives in search of Somali infiltrators. In truth, we were scrounging for anything that could be of use to our families: flour, cooking oil, dried beef, aspirin, bandages. Most of the time we bought the items, but sometimes we were able to trade them for some service or other. We spent afternoons in the shade, chewing *quat*, a mild stimulant that is also an effective appetite suppressant. I would go back to Mam and the kids with the morning's bounty and return once, before sunset, to take stock of their needs.

I usually took meals with my new friends, but sometimes I ate with my family. The food Mam offered us was typical refugee camp fare: stale bread and soup prepared from dried lentils or beans. Meals became sacred to us. They required our complete and undivided attention. One's mind was occupied only by the sensation of each small bite of stale bread as it broke against the teeth, by the barely discernible taste of watery soup. These meals were exercises in the detection of small differences: today, a tiny pinch of salt in the bean soup; tomorrow, a slightly better grade of water. If the soup was brown, it was because the water was brown.

Mealtime never passed without disruptions from unwelcome visitors, however. Vultures carved circles in the sky. Flies hovered above our plates.

Flies had always been part of my life. The flies that I knew in Jijiga were shy, timid creatures. They were hardly upstanding citizens, but they were still accepted as part of the family—every family. They slept on the bed, used the washroom, partook in family funerals. They never said thank you for the food they ate, but they knew when to retire: you needed only to wink an eye and they were gone. During the exodus, however, these winged creatures became so aggressive, so outrageously arrogant, that they required a good spanking before they would so much as stretch a wing.

Beetles and bugs could get into pots hung from the moon. They were a terrible nuisance, scurrying onto your plate, reminding you that even your watery bowl of soup had already been another's meal. Throwing

Nega Mezlekia

anything out was unthinkable. Eating it while you knew that it had already been tasted was repulsive. But hunger demanded compromises. The beetles received a spoonful of the territory they had claimed, and you worked to keep the rest.

Still, the food ran out a few days after we left Jijiga. We were still camped in the valley, hoping to return home, when the last cup of dried lentils was emptied into the cooking pot, the grain bag folded and placed in the storage sack. There was a flourishing black market in food, but only the very rich could afford to participate.

The army decided to help. It identified the profiteers responsible for the black market monopoly on flour, cooking oil, and salt. The guilty were brought before us, their hands tied behind them, as a reminder that the enemy was also within. Most of them were familiar faces: merchants from the Gurage ethnic group, well known for its entrepreneurs. It didn't surprise me that some unscrupulous merchants considered the exodus just another business opportunity, a once-in-a-lifetime chance to make a fast buck. I was even sympathetic. Who wouldn't be tempted to exploit such an unprecedented opportunity? But since I was one of their victims—since the traders' prices determined whether I would survive—I was also enraged. I was glad that they were to be shamed in public.

It was a beautiful desert morning. The air was still and cool, and the sun had just broken over the cliffs. The valley was peaceful; Ethiopian bombers had rained napalm on enemy territory the day before. Just after dawn, eleven men were lined up against the cliff walls and shot dead. They were the unscrupulous merchants. Some thought that the execution was a noble idea; perhaps the survivors would learn their lesson. As it turned out, the markets dried up altogether. There was no flour to be had, no cooking oil, no dried beef—nothing. No one would admit to ever having been a merchant. The ones who benefited from this drastic measure were the soldiers, who divided the confiscated goods among themselves. But soon the supplies were eaten up, and even they became victims of their brutal judgment.

Two days passed, and I had not had anything to eat. I chewed *quat.* The acidic juice of the leafy plant burned holes in my stomach, heart, and spirit. I drank water to extinguish the fire building up inside of me, but the warm liquid stirred up something in my stomach; I felt terribly nauseated.

I tried to stand up, but my head spun. My vision blurred. I couldn't find my legs.

I decided to quit chewing *quat* until I found something to eat. I sipped a bit of water from time to time and lay underneath an acacia tree. Hunger was nothing new to me. My life had been punctuated by episodes of hunger, thirst, and want. What I could not get used to was the hunger inside of hunger, that brief moment of ravenousness that came after your stomach had falsely promised to go without food.

Looking around, all I could see were vultures and weeds. I wondered where the gazelles had gone, the antelopes and spurfowls. This was not the Ogaden I knew. It was a different realm, a place where humans had squeezed all the vivacity out of the earth. I wished I was a bird.

Not surprisingly, the hunger was particularly tough on my three-year-old brother Henok, the youngest of the seven children in our family. The boy cried himself to sleep. After the second day without food it seemed that he would never wake up again. Mam soaked a rag in water and squeezed it between his chapped lips. She told him stories and promised him that soon he would have all the food he could eat, but he did not seem to hear.

I knew that I had to get the boy something to eat, and soon, or I would never see him again. Abraha, my officer friend, thought he could help. Abraha had been exempted from duty at the front ever since he had been wounded. He recovered much of his health during a stay in Jijiga, but the war had left him with a bad leg and only three fingers on his left hand. He still served in the army, but in a much humbler position. He spent most of his time with us, his civilian buddies. The young officer had come to terms with the fact that life in uniform was no longer for him; he planned to go to college and become a teacher as soon as the war ended. Abraha wasn't married, but his older sister had been widowed by the war, and she and her three children relied on him. While in Jijiga, he had visited her family often, disciplining her two young boys. Now, he also had to see that they did not starve to death or wander into minefields.

Abraha must have been gone a long time, because the sun was staring me in the face when I opened my eyes. I decided to get up and stretch my legs, but I was too weak.

My officer friend had returned, bearing a large loaf of bread, three cans of corned beef, and four bags of intravenous fluids—saline water and glucose. He mixed a potion out of these fluids and gave it to me. He opened a can and handed me some odd-tasting meat. It didn't take long before I was able to walk. The two of us took the rest to Mam and the kids.

The loaf of bread attracted many eyes. Desperate mothers stopped me along the way to beg a piece for their withering children. Some offered to pay, and dearly. But I did not have much to spare. Mam shot out of her seat when she saw the staff of life and hugged me, her fragile body unsteady and trembling. While holding Henok's sleeping body close to her chest, she bowed and thanked the officer with an awkwardness I have seldom seen in her.

The exodus killed more civilians than soldiers. Many people were killed or maimed as they walked, torn apart by antipersonnel mines buried underneath roads and jungle trails. Many more were killed by the cannon fire.

The cannons were predictable. They began slowly in the morning, ceasing altogether at lunch. The Somalis, we surmised, were chewing *quat*. The stimulant seemed to sharpen their senses, bringing on a predictable fit of frenzied artillery fire around three o'clock. At first, the targets were military supplies and personnel, but eventually the destruction became random. After a while, people no longer tried to dodge the bombs; they just went on with their daily chores.

About a week after we left Jijiga, as I lay in the afternoon shade, my friends reminded me that it was my turn to fetch water. By the time I arrived, the line extended for a quarter mile. I hoped that this would be one of those days when the army would bring extra water trucks, making it possible to shower as well. The dark dust had caked into a thin layer over my skin, and it was impossible to tell the color of my shirt. The sound of explosions interrupted my reverie. The cannons were right on schedule.

After I filled my jerrican with water and balanced it on my shoulder, I headed back through the crowd. Soldiers were dashing to and fro like mad ants. Women cried. Small groups had formed here and there, watch-

ing the smoldering smoke. I realized that the Somalis had done significant damage this time.

A circle of people had gathered at our resting place. I had to push my
way through. But my possessions had disappeared. The Jeep was gone,
the tree, my friends . . . surely I was lost. Then I realized that one of the
shells had landed right inside our small bit of shade, and all three of my
friends had perished. Their remains were scattered over a large area, min-
gled with ragged shreds of metal.

I was not shocked. I was not angry. I did not cry. I didn't feel lucky for
having survived, either. Strange as it may seem, I almost felt relieved for
them. Wherever they were now, I knew it couldn't be worse than the life
they had left.

I took the jerrican to Mam. She had already been to the site, and she
was visibly shaken. Tears streaked her dusty face. I had no words to offer
her. I found some shade nearby and sat alone, watching as the dispos-
sessed walked up and down, up and down. Everyone was carrying a
gun—young and old, rich and poor, Muslim and Christian, sick and
healthy. Stranger still, those who carried these guns were for the most
part unable to afford a single meal. A bag of flour cost forty dollars—a sol-
dier's monthly salary—but ten dollars could get you a slightly used Kalashnikov. If you bargained, they might even give you a hand grenade.

On the night of the explosion, it rained for the first time in well over
four years. Children had been born and raised without ever knowing the
touch of rain on their faces. Now they were mesmerized, ecstatic. The sky
lit up with fire, heaved and shook. And the children discovered that the
heavens were not about to swallow them up or break their tiny bodies:
the sky would pour water down on them—dear, precious water.

It rained for hours. There was no shelter from the rain, but it didn't
matter. The rain opened the people's hearts, brought out a faith that none
believed they still possessed. The storm was harsh, accompanied by hail
and wind, yet it was considered a good omen. All agreed that God had
opened the heavens so that our sins would be washed away along with
the filth, the rot, the stench of the camps. The future had been remade
into something bright, something clean and forgiving.

The next morning the settlement was eerily silent. Dawn broke quietly for the first time in memory. It was as though the rain had affected

the Somali soldiers with the same heavenly thoughts as us. We scrambled to leave the valley as soon as there was enough light to find our way. The effect of these sudden storms is often felt hours after they have stopped, when the accumulated rainfall gathers enough momentum to sweep away everything in its course. It is not unusual for a storm in southern Ethiopia to whisk trucks and buses away like specks of dirt on the bathtub floor.

That day twenty thousand of us walked until sunset. By then we were out of sniper range: the flood had gone behind us, sweeping across the valley, creating an insurmountable divide between the enemy and us. The rains had washed away the remains of my three friends, then built up into a huge force which created a chasm between Jijiga and Harar, saving our lives in the process. The next day we rested our sore bodies and ate our first decent meal in days. We were on the fringes of the highlands; we could buy fruit, milk, and other foods we had almost forgotten.

But Henok had been coughing for days, and he was having difficulty breathing. A knowledgeable nurse diagnosed him with asthma, reassuring my mother that the condition was not life threatening; indeed, since Henok was so young, it might even heal with time. Mam kept him warm by wrapping him with her *netela* at night, and she massaged his chest whenever he began to wheeze.

Four days after the miraculous storm, we finally arrived in the city of Harar. Those four days were uneventful. No one was killed or seriously injured. We knew then that the rain had indeed been a good omen. It had written itself into the people as well as the land.

Rhina P. Espaillat

You Call Me by Old Names

From *Callaloo*

You call me by old names: how strange
to think of "family" and "blood,"
walking through flakes, up to the knees
in cold and democratic mud.

And suddenly I think of people
dead many centuries ago:
my ancestors, who never knew
the dubious miracle of snow....

Don't say my names, you seem to mock
their charming, foolish Old World touch—
call me "immigrant," Social
Security card such-and-such,

or future citizen, who boasts
two eyes, two ears, a nose, a mouth,
but no names from another life,
a long time back, a long way south.

Danzy Senna

The Color of Love

From *O, The Oprah Magazine*

We had this much in common: We were both women, and we were both writers. But we were as different as two people can be and still exist in the same family. She was ancient—as white and dusty as chalk—and spent her days seated in a velvet armchair, passing judgments on the world be-low. She still believed in noble bloodlines; my blood had been mixed at conception. I believed there was no such thing as nobility or class or lin-eage, only systems designed to keep some people up in the big house and others outside, in the cold.

She was my grandmother. She was Irish but from that country's Prot-estant elite, which meant she seemed more British than anything. She was an actress, a writer of plays and novels and still unmarried in her thir-ties when she came to America to visit. One night while in Boston, she went to a dinner party, where she was seated next to a young lawyer with blood as blue as the ocean. Her pearl earring fell in his oyster soup—or so the story goes—and they fell in love. My grandmother married that law-yer and left her native Ireland for New England.

How she came to have black grandchildren is a story of opposites. It was 1968 in Boston when her daughter—my mother—a small, blonde Wasp poet, married my father, a tall and handsome black intellectual, in an act that was as rebellious as it was hopeful. The products of that unlikely union—my older sister, my younger brother and I—grew up in urban chaos, in a home filled with artists and political activists. The old lady across the river in Cambridge seemed to me an endangered species. Her walls were covered with portraits of my ancestors, the pale and dead men who had conquered Africa and built Boston long before my time. When I visited, their eyes followed me from room to room with what I imagined to be an expression of scorn. Among the portraits sat my grandmother, a bird who had flown in to remind us all that there had indeed been a time when lineage and caste meant something. To me, young and dark and full of energy, she was the missing link between the living and the dead.

But her blood flowed through me, whether I liked it or not. I grew up to be a writer, just like her. And as I struggled to tell my own stories—about race and class and post–civil rights America—I wondered who my grandmother had been before, in Dublin, when she was friend and confidante to literary giants such as William Butler Yeats and Samuel Beckett. Once, while snooping in her bedroom, I discovered her novels, the ones that had been published in Ireland when she was my age. I stared at her photograph on the jacket and wondered about the young woman who wore a mischievous smile. Had she ever worried about becoming so powerful that no man would want her? Did she now feel that she had sacrificed her career and wild Irishwoman dreams to become a wife and mother and proper Bostonian?

I longed to know her—to love her. But the differences between us were real and alive, and they threatened to squelch our fragile connection. She was an alcoholic. In the evening, after a few glasses of gin, she could turn vicious. Though she held antiquated racist views, my grandmother would still have preferred to see my mother married and was saddened when my parents split in the seventies. She believed that a woman without a man was pitiable. The first question she always asked me when she saw me: "Do you have a man?" The second question: "What is he?" That was her way of finding out his race and background. She looked visibly pleased if he was a Wasp, neutral if he was Jewish and disappointed if he was black.

My mother ignored her hurtful comments but felt them just the same. She spent her visits to my grandmother's house slamming dishes

Danzy Senna

in the kitchen, hissing her anger just out of hearing range, then raving, on the drive home, about what awful thing her mother had said this time. Like my mother, I knew the rule: I was not to disrespect elders. She was old and gray and would soon be gone. But I had inherited my grandmother's short temper. When I got angry, even as a child, I felt as if blood were rushing around in my head, red waves battering the shore. Words spilled from my mouth—cutting, vicious words that I regretted.

One autumn day in Cambridge, at my grandmother's place, I lost my temper. I was home from college for the holidays, staying in her guest room. I woke from a nap to the sound of her enraged voice shouting at what I could only imagine was the television.

"Idiot! You damn fool!" she bellowed. "You stupid, stupid woman!" It has to be *Jeopardy!*, I thought. She must be yelling at those tiny contestants on the screen. She knows the answers to those questions better than they do. But when the shouting went on for a beat too long, I went to the top of the stairs and looked down into the living room. She was speaking to a real person: her cleaning lady, a Greek woman named Mary, who was on her hands and knees, nervously gathering the shards of a broken vase. My grandmother stood over her, hands on hips, cursing.

"You fool," my grandmother repeated. "How in bloody hell could you have done something so stupid?"

"Grandma." I didn't shout her name but said it loudly enough that she, though hard of hearing, glanced up.

"Oh, darling!" she piped, suddenly cheerful. "Would you like a cup of tea? You must be dreadfully tired."

Mary was on her feet again. She smiled nervously at me, then rushed into the kitchen with the pieces of the broken vase.

I told myself to be a good girl, to be polite. But something snapped. I marched down the stairs, and even she noticed something on my face that made her sit in her velvet chair.

"Don't you ever talk to her that way," I shouted. "Where do you think you are? Slavery was abolished long ago."

I stood over her, tall and long-limbed, daring her to speak. My grandmother shook her head. "It's about race, isn't it?"

"Race?" I said, baffled. "Mary's white. This is about respect—treating other human beings with respect."

She wasn't hearing me. All she saw was color. "The tragedy about you," she said soberly, "is that you are mixed." I felt those waves in my head: "Your tragedy is that you're old and ignorant," I spat. "You don't know the first thing about me."

She cried into her hands. She seemed diminished, a little old woman. She looked up only to say, "You are a cruel girl."

I left her apartment trembling yet feeling exhilarated by what I had done. But my elation soon turned to shame. I had taken on an old lady. And for what? Her intolerance was, at her age, deeply entrenched. My rebuttals couldn't change her.

Yet that fight marked the beginning of our relationship. I've since decided that when you cease to express anger toward those who have hurt you, you are essentially giving up on them. They are dead to you. But when you express anger, it is a sign that they still matter, that they are worth the fight.

After that argument, my grandmother and I began a conversation. She seemed to see me clearly for the first time, or perhaps she, a "cruel girl" herself, had simply met her match. And I no longer felt she was a relic. She was a living, breathing human being who deserved to be spoken to as an equal.

I began visiting her more. I would drive to Cambridge and sit with her, eating mixed nuts and sipping ginger ale, regaling her with tales of my latest love drama or writing project. In her presence, I was proudly black and young and political, and she was who she was: subtly racist, terribly elitist and awfully funny. She still said things that angered me: She bemoaned my mother's marriage to my father, she said that I should marry not for love but for money, and she told me that I needn't identify as black, since I didn't look it. I snapped back at her. But she, with senility creeping in, didn't seem to hear me; each time I came, she said the same things.

Last summer I went into hiding to work on my second novel at a writers' retreat in New Hampshire. The place was a kind of paradise for creative souls, a hideaway where every writer had his or her own cabin in the woods with no phone or television—no distractions to speak of. But I was miserable. I could not write. Even the flies outside my window

Danzy Senna

seemed to whisper, "Go out and play. Forget the novel. Leave it till tomorrow."

I woke one morning at four, the light outside my window still blue. I felt panic and sadness, though I didn't know why. I got up, dressed and went outside for a walk through the forest. But the panic persisted, and I began to cry. I assumed that my writer's block had seized me suddenly.

That night I ate dinner in the main house and received a call on the pay phone from my mother. She told me my grandmother had fallen and broken her leg. But that wasn't all; she had subsequently suffered a heart attack. Her other organs were failing. I had to hurry if I wanted to say good-bye.

I drove to Boston that night, not believing that we could be losing her. She would make it. I was certain. Sure, she was ninety-two, frail, unable to walk steadily. But she was lucid, and her tongue was as sharp as ever. Somehow I had imagined her as indestructible, made immortal by power and cruelty and wit.

The woman I found in the hospital bed was barely recognizable. My grandmother had always been fussy about her appearance. She never showed her face without makeup. Even in the day, when it was just she and the cleaning lady, she dressed as if she were ready for a cocktail party. At night she usually had cocktail parties; doddering old men hovered around her, sipping Scotch and bantering about theater and politics.

My grandmother's face had swollen to twice its normal size, and tubes came out of her nose. She had struggled so hard to pull them out that the nurses had tied her wrists to the bed rails. Her hair was gray and thin. Her body was withered and bruised, barely covered by the green hospital gown.

Her hazel eyes were all that was still recognizable, but the expression in them was different from any I had ever seen on her—terror. She was terrified to die. She tried to rise when she saw me, and her eyes pleaded with me to help her, to save her, to get her out of this mess. I stood over her, and I felt only one thing: overwhelming love. Not a trace of anger. That dark gray rage I'd felt toward her was gone as I stroked her forehead and told her she would be okay, even knowing she would not.

For two days, my mother, her sisters and I stood beside my grandmother, singing Irish ballads and reading passages to her from the works of her favorite novelist, James Joyce. For the first time, she could not talk. At one point, she gestured wildly for pen and paper. I brought her the pen and the paper and held them up for her, but she was too weak for even that. What came out was only a faint, incomprehensible line.

In death we are each reduced to our essence: the spirit we are when we are born. The trappings we hold on to our whole lives—our race, our money, our sex, our age, our politics—become irrelevant. My grandmother became a child in that hospital bed, a spirit about to embark on an unknown journey, terrified and alone, no matter how many of us were crowded around her. In the final hours, even her skin seemed to lose its wrinkles and take on a waxy glow. Then, finally, the machines around us went silent as she left us behind to squabble in the purgatory of the flesh.

Cornelius Eady

How to Do

From *U.S. Latino Review*

It embarrasses my niece to think of her mother
Walking the streets with a cart
Picking up empties
For their deposits,

But my sister knows how to do
Which was all our mother asked of us.
She's learned how to do,
Which is both a solution and a test,

So I stand in line with my sister
At the supermarket.
Today's the best day of the week
To bring the bottles in.

It is a poor people's science,
A concept that works until
Someone with power
Notices it works,

And then, it doesn't.
There's at least 15 carts,
At least 10 people in line,

But only one guy
Behind the counter:
Not what's supposed
To happen.

The manager shrugs
His shoulders when asked.
No rules here,

Points to a sign taped
Above our heads
Which, boiled down,
Says wait, behave.

No rules, except for
What's always been:
Do what you gotta do.

And the poor stiff
Whose job it is to sort the clears
From the greens, the plastics
From the cans, who is short
One or two people this shift,

Who flings my sister's
Stumpy treasure
Into the hamper's
Great indifferent mouth,
Temporary chief of staff
Of Lotto,

Who's been instructed to keep
The refunds down to
Twelve dollars' worth of
Store credit, no matter
How many empties
Come in,

Maybe he has a favorite song.
Maybe he's a good guy
To have in a pinch.
He's not paid enough to reveal that here.

This, as my mother would say,
Is the way we have to do:
Tired as convicts, we inch along,
Shift our weight
On the black,
Sticky carpet,

Beholden to nobodies luck
But our own.

Dagoberto Gilb

I Knew She Was Beautiful

From *The New Yorker*

I was holding her hand at a train depot. I can still feel my arm in the air, limp and soft with trust. It must have been Union Station, Los Angeles, and I don't know where we were going or why. I was thrilled. I was small, probably just walking, and looking up at her I swear I knew then that she was beautiful. She was wearing a hat, one of those brimless hats women wore in the fifties that matched the rest of the outfit. There was a red rose in the hat, I'm sure. It wasn't a real rose but a lacy decorative one. Almost all my other early images of her are from the department stores we used to go to together. She's trying clothes on, everybody paying attention to her, or standing at a cosmetics counter, my mommy and the women around talking fast and unashamed, giggling, playing with the silver and gold and glass tubes, the jars and sprays, the smallest brushes, the colored powders. The train depot on that trip was the black-and-white of a dream, and the indoors had the faraway feel of the outdoors, its expanse as dusty as a memory.

I think it was La Cienega. It was a Spanish name, and the other stores where she modelled—downtown or on Wilshire Boulevard, department stores like the Broadway and Robinson's—didn't have Spanish names. The store didn't seem large. Just elegant. Racks of women's clothes with beads and jewels, collars and sleeves, strings and straps and bows, low in the front, low in the back. I went into the dressing room, where all the models were changing from one thing into another for the show that day. I watched them, breathing the cool mist of perfume, as they hurried through the step-throughs and pull-offs of dress and undress—the zippers and snaps, the gritty static or smooth wisp of on and off. Skin that was legs and arms, and round hips that cut into small waists; bras, even a breast, and panties that showed that darkened mystery hair. The piccolo of women's voices. I was a good boy, they said. I would be such a handsome man. I remember the warmth of their touch, like that of my favorite blanket. I used to scissor my fingers onto its nylon end-seam to go to sleep, my thumb in my mouth, sucking. Even then I knew it was women, their attraction and allure, that I loved, *mi* mommy and her friends, her best friend, the woman from Puerto Rico who she could whisper to in Spanish. But it was this day I remember because on the other side of the store there was an old man in a uniform tinting a display window that faced the street. There were mannequins behind him and he let me go through a half door to sit between him and them. He brushed on the tint, the glass becoming a yellow brown, that biting, tart odor, and I looked out at the people and cars passing by on the other side of the window. I would run from him back to the dressing room, from one scent to the other, back and forth, the fumes subliminal and intoxicating as I ran from the old man with the paintbrush and can in the room no one got to sit in to the beautiful women in their underwear.

She loved to go to Hollywood Park, and we went to the last race because admission was free. I loved to go, too, and not just because of the horses, the earth shuddering under me as they left the gate and pounded across the finish line. I liked to collect the bet stubs like baseball cards, the losers thrown down, a trail of litter that began in the parking lot until it carpeted the grandstands. I collected fives and tens, win, place, or show. Win stubs were the hardest to find. Wandering the track was like walking on a beach looking for unbroken shells. We'd go down to the general-admission area, at track level, or we'd walk right over to a nicer area, where there were chairs and tables and drinks, and sometimes we were invited to sit in a private glass-enclosed clubhouse. A man would offer to buy us drinks, and I'd get a Roy Rogers—grenadine and Coke. She gave me the green olives on toothpicks from her drink to eat. The man who bought the drinks might say something at a distance first, and then approach. Usually, she just told a waiter, or the man himself, thank you so much, polite, generously happy about the drinks, but that would be it, and there we'd be, her and me at the races. I was her date. I was her man. Those men, in their suits and their blazers, snugged or loosened ties, stinking in their colognes, snapping bills off silver money clips, they were obvious, stupid, easy even for me to figure out. She might light a cigarette. She didn't smoke, though, for the taste. It was a look she wanted. I'd complain that I couldn't find betting stubs. She'd tell me to look around where we were sitting, and I'd search the tops of the starched tablecloths, the ashtrays, hunting the big losers. One time, I found four hundred-dollar tickets to win, creased the long way.

She was seeing this one man. Years later, I learned that she'd been seeing him for some time, even before she and my father divorced, which was soon after I was born. His voice was loud by design, the way a horn is loud. She used to ask me, Do you like him? He took us to baseball games. The Tigers and Angels and Yankees, the Dodgers and Giants and Pirates. The year Roger Maris hit sixty-one home runs I caught one of his B.P. homers. The loud man let me hang around after the games and get autographs. He was a big man, a fireman, and sometimes we visited him at his station. I was too scared to slide down the pole. It was too fat, too thick. I played handball alone in a white room beside the red trucks. He wasn't a bad man, but I didn't like him very much. I couldn't explain why, except that he was loud when he talked, and even though he bought me ice cream anytime I wanted it, he was no fun. And so I would answer her. No, I would say.

We were in the kitchen. I was sitting in one of those heavy metal chairs with glossy vinyl covering—we had two of them—and my mom got mad at me. I was used to this. She had a job now in a dental office, and things like this happened because she was tired when she came home. But this time he was there. They were always going out, and I was left at home alone with our knobless television and a TV dinner, sometimes two, because I was getting taller, flexing muscles I could see in my arms. He only came inside our house once in a while, and she must have told me to go away, to get out of the kitchen. In that loud voice he told me to

Dagoberto Gilb

do what she said. I sat there. Then he was louder, really yelling. I sat there. And so he grabbed me and I held onto the metal rails under the chair and he picked it up along with me. I'm not leaving! I told him. You don't tell me! He was furious, and my mom was yelling now, too, and she told him to leave me alone, and he stopped, dropping the chair and me in it. I went into the bedroom and I was crying, waiting for her to come. She hit me sometimes, and when she got there that's what I was expecting. Instead she held me and she was smiling. She was proud of me. She said, You're such a man already.

At school the kids said things. I knew it. I was bigger than they were and more athletic, and angry all the time, and it wasn't like they were going to say anything much to my face. My mom was a Mexican and my mom was divorced, and one time a girl told me her mom didn't like mine and she didn't like me, either. I didn't hang out with too many kids. There was this one boy—he had his own bedroom, with toys everywhere. He had a basketball, and a hoop on the garage. I would want to play, but he was soft, blubbery, and I'd shoot alone for as long as his mom would let me. She was always smoking and drinking coffee in a stained white mug and talking on the phone, and once I came over and she took me into their clean bathroom and got a washcloth and washed my neck and behind my ears, scrubbed so hard it hurt. She was supposed to be a friend of my mom's, but I knew she wasn't, not really, because whenever my mom came to collect me only my mom talked.

Sometimes my mom would take me to the Food Giant and buy me a chili dog with finely grated cheese on the top that would melt in a minute. When she went out, which was a lot, she left me some money and I'd ride a bike down to the Thrifty and buy a half-gallon square of chocolate ice cream. She didn't cook, except on my birthday, when she made *chile verde* that stewed for hours. She'd buy tamales from a bakery on Whittier Boulevard. In the morning, before she went to work and I went to school, we had breakfast at a coffee shop, and she'd give me her hash-brown potatoes. Even then, at that hour, men looked at her. Even then, men would come up to our table, squat so that they could talk to her. Introduce themselves. I was starting junior high, I had touched a girl, looked at nudie magazines, and I knew what these men wanted. I was such a good-looking boy, they would tell her. When they guessed at my age, they missed by years, and then the talk would be about her beauty—how could such a young woman have a son so old? She was too polite to them, and one time I remember this man's eyes looking at my mom. I wanted us to be alone. I didn't want her to be polite. I was so mad at her. I was so mad then that I think I never got over it.

She'd stopped modelling, but when she and her Puerto Rican friend got together they talked about the other models' getting fat butts and saggy *chiches*, girdles and falsies. Her Puerto Rican friend was marrying a man who owned the biggest sailboat ever and they were going around the world in it. He was so rich he didn't have to work. My mom had to work. It made her tired. She was going out on more dates, too, so she was always busy. She talked wistfully about Pancho Gonzalez, the tennis star. Another friend of hers was supposed to be his cousin. She was a woman who talked too fast and too much, and she drank, and she laughed wrong. She and my mom both bleached their hair platinum, but this friend's was ugly and cheap-looking. She was a *fea*, short and plump and pimply, but she thought she was as pretty as my mom. She was bad news, I knew, because by then I was smarter than my mom seemed to be. This "cousin" did not help my mom win Pancho Gonzalez, but they got drunk a lot together. My mom's Puerto Rican friend stopped coming around. Maybe she was sailing on the Pacific Ocean, maybe not yet, but she was married, and she was rich, and we weren't.

Though the modelling jobs weren't around anymore, the pretty clothes were. Bills came in the mail daily. I answered the phone and a bill collector would ask for her and I'd say she wasn't home even if she was. She was working for a dentist who was a Mormon, and she was dating him, too, and two old biddies started coming to our door lecturing my mom, and I listened to them with her. I answered their questions because she didn't know the answers. She wanted to become a Mormon, she didn't care how. We went to the dentist's house for Thanksgiving, my first Thanksgiving dinner. His mother had a bun of white and gray hair and a frilly apron just like one of those grandmothers on a TV show. We had to sit at a long dinner table, crowded with people. It was a feast of full bowls and platters, and I ate so much turkey and mashed potatoes that I got sick, but I didn't think it was because I overate. It was because they didn't

Dagoberto Gilb

like my mom. Well, I didn't like these people from the start. My mom and I spoke to each other, and they looked at us as if we were being secretive, as if we were talking in Spanish, not in English. After dinner we were taking a walk around the neighborhood with the dentist—it was green with overgrown trees and grass, and there weren't always sidewalks, and the idea was that he should get to know me a little—when my mom said that something was wrong, she was bleeding. She assured me it wasn't that kind of bleeding, teased me for not understanding immediately, but he didn't laugh. He didn't like this, didn't want to have to find an open store, couldn't believe she wouldn't be prepared. She sloughed that off, wanting to be cheerful. She wanted to make him happy. But he didn't laugh. This was the man I'd been lying about to new junior-high friends. Before I met him, my mom had told me that she was going to marry him. My dad, I'd tell these guys, snooty, was a dentist. I wanted us to be richer than them. After that day I don't remember ever hearing her talk about him again, and I never asked.

Two or three times my mom took me to an old lady's house. It was an old house, with old things, and I had to have good manners and eat boring food. The woman thought I was a bright boy and liked it when I visited, my mom told me, and I might be getting an inheritance from her. When the old lady died, I went to the funeral parlor with my mom to pay last respects. There were no other people there, and still I felt as though we were being watched like thieves. The casket was open, but I didn't look close. It was like a church, with wooden pews and crosses and Jesuses, though no Virgins. My mom's knees went onto the padded kneel board, and as they did she made a loud *pedo*. I don't think I'd ever heard that from her before. She looked at me and I looked at her and we both tried to hold back from laughing. The more we did, the worse it hurt, and the stronger was the desire to laugh. She kept kneeling there, her hands folded and her head down as though she were praying, but really she was giggling and then we both started laughing too hard. There was no inheritance for either of us.

One night I was watching TV when a man who my mom worked for, someone I think she'd also gone out with, came to the door screaming about her. She was out on a date. He was wailing about money, what had she done with his money. He was drunk and howling and cussing. I knew about drunk because sometimes there were bottles in the house, broken glasses, laughter. I knew who this man was because he'd shot someone. Mom had told me about him, and I'd heard her tell her friends. He kept beating on the door, and it finally blew open right in front of me just as a cop neighbor I'd called came running up. A week later she married a man raised near Lancaster. I'd never heard of him, I'd never met him before. He was the cousin of a woman she'd worked with. He had the stupidest grin, as stupid as his hick name. He asked me if there was one thing he could do for me. I said I wanted him to take me to see Washington, D.C., and he grinned that dumb grin and said he would. I actually believed him. He and my mom went to Arizona for a week for their honeymoon, and after that we moved in. He wore a different clean green uniform every day for his job, and most of the rest of the time, too. There were deer heads and birds and fish on the walls. Maple furniture, a family table with matching chairs. He had a son who was a taxidermist, and he was proud of him. My mom's new husband was an electrician and a couple of times I worked for him and that's when I heard him tell his working friends he just felt so lucky to be married to such a pretty Mexican gal. A few weeks later she went on the TV show "Let's Make a Deal" and she was chosen. When Monty Hall asked her name, she told him her new name without a flinch. But she didn't win anything big—twenty or forty bucks, that was all— and she didn't get to pick a door.

Not too long afterward, she asked me to go to lunch with her. We hadn't gone out together, the two of us, for some time because she was so busy with her new husband. They were beginning to have arguments about bills and money, and they raced to get the mail first. The lunch wasn't only with my mom. It was with the loud man, the fireman, she'd dated before. He took us to a restaurant. I don't remember the food, only that when he pulled into the driveway of the apartment building where we lived, she jumped out of the car and rushed to the front door, and I was stuck in the back seat and this old boyfriend leaned over to talk to me. He told me he loved my mom and he was sorry and he wished something or other, I don't know. It was a speech, and it seemed as if he might cry or already was crying, but I told him I had to go. Maybe this was why I didn't like him. Big as he was, he was too loud, and yet he would cry. I think the car was a Thunderbird coupe, and I didn't even enjoy that. Things weren't good between my mom and her husband, and I knew she wasn't happy— I figured that she'd been sneaking out for these lunches with the fireman for a while—but I started avoiding my mom and her husband as much as possible. I never liked the deer meat or the maple furniture or the Hank Snow music, and I ate with my new neighborhood friends, stayed as late as I could. Then my mom and her husband separated, and we moved to an apartment complex on the south side of town. She would just lie on the couch, half awake, half asleep, depressed. We didn't talk too much. I had a job, and even though I was getting in fights at school and she was getting calls from the vice-principal about suspensions and swats and the rest, she didn't really care, and I didn't think it was such a big deal, either.

She married the loud fireman, who was almost ten years younger than she was—though nobody ever thought so—and who loved her after all this time. He bought her a brand-new house and everything that went in it, and it was as if we were rich, though I didn't feel as though anything was mine. It was all theirs. His and hers. He wasn't there very much. He worked hard at two jobs—he drove a Brink's truck, too—and she had all the money she'd ever dreamed of because he gave her his paychecks as if she were a financial wizard. When we were alone, or when she was joking in front of the women who would visit, she would say that he could be boring and dull, and that if he wasn't gone most of the time, if she didn't keep him working two jobs ... Then she'd laugh, and everyone laughed with her. She always had food, and always a drink. There were jugs of wine and there was beer and liquor. There was a new blender, the best. He loved to drink with her, too. He loved everything she did, everything she bought, and she bought everything. She was the best thing that he could ever imagine happening to him, his life was full of sunlight and colors he'd never seen. I wasn't around much, going back to my old friends in my old high school, going to a new job to have my own money, partying myself now, playing with drugs and liquor and girlfriends, but I was happy that she wasn't worried anymore. Since she didn't have to do anything but please him, she pleased him. He didn't like "spicy" food, so she learned to cook potatoes and roasts. She babied him when he got home, made him feel like he ran the world. They drank together. They talked to each other and had fun when they drank. When she was around him, she became like him. When he thought he should be serious, he droned philosophically about black people and illegal aliens. My mom was an illegal alien, born out of wedlock in Mexico City and baptized at the Basílica Santa María de Guadalupe. She often tried to stop him when he went off on a long editorial, but it wasn't always worth it to her.

My mother was becoming a person I wouldn't want to know, and sometimes, especially when I was reminding her of a past that she didn't want to remember, she'd get mad. Once I told a neighbor that her husband wasn't my real father. I didn't know that I wasn't supposed to say this. I was sorry I embarrassed her. I didn't even care about my real father much, I only saw him a couple of days a year, but the only times my mother's husbands were fathers were when others made that assumption. They were just men to me, part of her life, not mine. Another time, after a year of living in this new house, with this new husband, I made her so angry by something I'd said or done, she told me she didn't know where I'd come from. She meant it, too, looking at me like I was an utter stranger, a lousy tenant.

On a Tuesday morning, just before dawn, I jerked myself out of a dream. It was so vivid I turned on a light and wrote it down. In the dream, a voice was talking to me, asking me if I wanted to talk to my mother. Why wouldn't I? Because we never did anymore, hadn't really talked in decades. When we did, there was nothing but awkwardness and mutual disapproval between us, and for several years there was nothing at all. I'd moved far away, to El Paso. The voice in the dream was asking me questions from my mother, and I started responding to the dream, to the voice, and straight to my mom. I answered the voice, yes, I always loved her. She had to know that I didn't care about whatever it was that had come between us, that I would remember only how much I loved her. I was always proud of her. I thought she was the best mommy, the most beautiful woman. I said I understood everything she'd gone through. Of course I didn't think only about the past, our troubles. Of course I forgave her, and I told her I wanted her to forgive me, too. And then I was overcome by a sob that wasn't in my dream but in my body and my mouth and my eyes.

Dagoberto Gilb

Two days later, her husband called me. He was calm and positive. My mom, he said, had been taken to the hospital Tuesday. She was found unconscious. There was a problem with her liver. She was in intensive care, but he was convinced she'd be home soon. He just thought I should know. I thought this sounded much more serious, and I called the hospital. A nurse there said I was right, usually it was only a matter of time, it could be at any moment, though it could also take days or even a few weeks. I asked about the liver, whether it was the usual reason a liver goes. She asked, Well, was she always the life of the party? I got a plane ticket. I remembered a previous visit, and finding an empty vodka bottle—plastic, the cheapest brand you could buy—in the corner of the bedroom where I was sleeping, and where she kept a mountain of purses and shoes and wallets. I found another, most of it gone, behind a closet door.

I rented a car at the airport and went to the hospital. She was bloated, her hair a tousle—a woman who never missed a hairdresser's appointment—an unappealing white gown tied around her. Tubes needled into her hand and arm, a clear mask was over her mouth and nose. When she heard me, her eyes opened. She had no voice. I talked. Years had passed, she knew little about my life. She knew that I did construction work, thought it was all I did, ever, didn't know anything about the other life I led, the one as a writer. I never told her. I was afraid that she would only be his wife, not my mom, and she wouldn't care in the appropriate way. Or that she would be too relieved, and that all those other years I'd been struggling, when she disapproved of me, even thought I deserved whatever misery befell me, would be forgotten. I didn't want to give that up so easily. These were the reasons I had told her nothing. But I knew my mom would be proud. I knew she would be happy for me. I told her that I was a writer, and that I'd had a book published, another one just out. I had been going to New York City and Washington, D.C. I'd gone there more than once, and I never paid. Her eyes smiled so big. I knew she would like this the most. She always wanted to travel the world. Can you believe they even give me money? I asked her. She was proud of me, and she was as surprised as I was about it. And then I told her why I had to come. I told her about the dream I'd had two nights before, on the first night she spent in the hospital. My mom's eyes stopped moving. I said, I talked to you, you were talking to me, we were talking. She nodded—her whole weakened body squirmed while she was nodding. I knew it, and yet I wouldn't believe this story if I'd heard it. It was such a *telenovela* deathbed scene, mother and son, both weeping about a psychic conversation routed hundreds of miles through the smog and traffic and over the mountains and across three deserts, from one dream to another, so that we wouldn't miss telling each other for the last time before she died. She was as stunned as I was, as happy. You know? She kept nodding, looking at me, crying. Oh, Mom, I said.

Dagoberto Gilb

Black Petal

From *DoubleTake*

I never claimed night fathered me.
That was my dead brother talking in his sleep.
I keep him under my pillow, a dear wish
that colors my laughing and crying.

I never said the wind, remembering nothing,
leaves so many rooms unaccounted for,
only continual farewell ransoms
the unmistakable fragrance
our human days afford.

It was my brother, little candle in the pulpit,
reading out loud to all of Earth
from the book of night.

He died too young to learn his name.
Now he answers to Vacant Boat,
Burning Wing, My Black Petal.

    *

Ask him who his mother is. He'll declare the birds
have eaten the path home, and each of us
joins night's ongoing story
wherever night overtakes him, the heart astonished
to find such fast belonging
and thanks answering thanks.

Ask if he's hungry or thirsty,
he'll say he's the bread come to pass
and draw you a map
to the twelve secret hips of honey.

Does anyone want to know the way to spring?
He'll remind you
the flower was never meant to survive
the fruit's triumph,
even as the fruit is meant for our cheer
under branches more ancient than the memory
of our grandmother's hair.

He says an apple's most secret cargo
is the enduring odor of a human childhood,
our mother's linen pressed and stored, our father's voice
walking through the rooms.

He says he's forgiven our sister
for playing dead and making him cry
those afternoons we were left alone in the house.

And when clocks frighten me with their long hair,
and when I spy the wind's numerous hands
in the orchard unfastening
first the petals from the buds,
then the perfume from the flesh,
          *

my dead brother ministers to me.
His voice weighs nothing but the far years
between stars in their massive dying,

and I grow quiet hearing how many
of both of our tomorrows lie waiting
inside it to be born.

Sonia Sanchez

A Poem for My Father

From *Callaloo*

how sad it must be
to love so many women
to need so many black
perfumed bodies weeping
underneath you.
      when i remember all those nights
i filled my mind with
long wars between short
sighted trojans & greeks
while you slapped some
wide hips about in
your pvt dungeon,
when i remember your
deformity   i want to
do something about your
makeshift manhood.
i guess
      that is why
on meeting your sixth
wife, i cross myself
with her confessionals.

Notes from the Catwalk

From *Creative Nonfiction*

I have worked as a stripper off and on for the last four years, mostly off for the last two, but recently I've returned. This latest stint began in December, and I told myself it would end with 1997—four weeks max, in and out; I would get that fast-flowing holiday cash and get out. New Year's came and New Year's went, and I'm still at it, an admission that brings me as much perverse pride as shame. Each return inspires a barnyard chorus of friends and family, people who care about me: "This is b-a-a-a-d." I don't disagree with them, but it's not that simple. I believe that most of us have our "netherlands"—subterranean places we visit to tap into our own pathology, resilience, and despair. The strip joint is an arena where I confront much of my own. I hope it will soon exhaust what it has to show me, but it hasn't yet.

I return during low points of my life, drawn like a child to what glitters instead of holding out for the warm and solid gold. I need the attention, the affection, the adulation. And the objectification and brutality just underneath? The strip joint is a sadomasochistic place, and sadomasochism is at the core of all my writing; it's the lens through which I see the world. For this reason, the job is endlessly interesting to me. There is an immediate change in lifestyle. I spend money: on gourmet coffee, luxurious bath products, taxis, takeout deliveries, a new coat. Walking past storefront windows, I feel as if the world has opened back up to me. If I'm at the grocery store, I don't have to agonize over whether I can afford the imported tomatoes. If I'm going to a party, I bring a bottle of good liquor and a dozen roses for the hostess.

I sleep a good part of the day and stay up all night, often well beyond the end of the night's work. My shift ends at four in the morning, and why stop there? I'll go to The Hellfire Club—an after-hours S&M establishment—for a free and thorough foot massage, and then to breakfast with strangers. There is a heightened sense of adventure, abandon, unreality. Day turns into night turns into next day.... I crash and then it's time to do it again.

I work in a club I'll call The Catwalk. It's in midtown, a few blocks northwest of Times Square. Sometimes on my way to work I imagine I'm an actress, or maybe a real dancer, who's gone too long between successful auditions. I walk past 42nd Street, under the big-time billboards, past the Broadway shows, then the off-Broadway shows, and finally into the strip club.

There is a bodily consolation in the entrance, that blast of heat as I come in from the cold (as Stephen Dunn put it, "What fools the body more than warmth?"). Too, the music at the door is like a wave that flattens all thought, washes it away. I am never without gratitude for its mindless, insistent rhythm; I become part of its pulse almost instantly. It pulls me out of myself and into Jo-Jo, my stripping persona.

The strip joint has a carnival atmosphere: seedy, raucous, lusty. The D.J. natters on like a barker all night long, calling girls to the stage, pushing the Champagne Lounge, casually insulting the customers ("Hey guys, do you remember your first blow job? How did it taste? Har!"). There is even a freak-show element: the feature performers with their engorged silicone breasts, boasting measurements like 101, 24, 36, who dance with snakes, fellate foot-long sausages, and the like.

A few words about how the place works:

The club does not pay the dancers to work there. The dancers pay the club: thirty dollars to the house, a ten-dollar minimum tip-out to the D.J. (double that if you want to be on his good side—and believe me, you do), and at least seven dollars to the housemother. All in all, including the taxi home, girls drop an average of seventy-five dollars a night to work in a club like The Catwalk, relying solely on the customers to make it back and more.

Dancers rotate on stage as called by the D.J. Each stage set is three songs; girls strip down to a g-string and heels by the end of the first. Between stage sets, the dancers circulate on the floor and attempt to sell private dances to customers at $10 a song. The girls are topless during these private dances, which consist mostly of teasing a man into a frenzy. At the height of frustration, some men will elect to visit the Champagne Lounge, a room upstairs where a customer can take his favorite girl. The Champagne Lounge is the ultimate scam. The hourly rate starts at $300, and this entitles the patron to exclusive time with the dancer of his choice and a bottle of champagne. Nothing special happens in there, though many customers imagine otherwise. I don't pretend to understand why anyone pays for it when they can open the Yellow Pages and find an escort for half the price. But dozens of men put their hundreds down every night and it's not unusual for them to buy more hours when the first one is up.

The Champagne Lounge is the strangest aspect of a very strange place. Here is a man I don't know, and I'm climbing into his lap, and he's cradling me. Sometimes this is all they want, and once in a while when I'm in the midst of such an encounter, everything falls away and I no longer remember how I got there. Only: he's hurting and I'm hurting and we're clinging to each other for this hour out of life. His arms are around me, strong male arms. My cheek is resting against the starched whiteness of his shirt. He rocks me, croons to me. This happens. I close my eyes and I am held. This is all I know; at this moment, all I need to know. All I need.

Each shift is something like an egg hunt. We're turned loose for the night at 8:00, and we convene in the dressing room again at 4:00 A.M., each girl with a different amount of money, bounty, depending on her calculations and effort and luck. The money is not discussed except in the vaguest of terms:

"How'd you do tonight?"

"Oh, I did all right. You?"

*

Strip-joint managers run a tight ship. The dress code is nonnegotiable. G-strings must be opaque, heels a minimum of four inches high. The only agony to match dancing in those stilettos for eight hours is the moment they come off: the effort to readjust to being flat-footed. (In this respect, they resemble tit clamps—the hot insistent bite while they're on; the excruciating rush of blood back into the nipple when they're removed.)

Tattoos must be covered; bodily piercings stripped of all jewelry; legs, armpits, and the bikini area kept clean-shaven or waxed. Garters are required, and each girl is expected to have several different costumes.

Dancers are not allowed to talk to each other while on stage. ("And I don't care what you're talkin' about. Just don't do it. Even if you're just tellin' another girl her tampon string's hangin' out. I don't know what you're talkin' about, and I'll make sure you get a five-song set.") Five-song sets are one way to torture a dancer. The stage is intended as a showcase, and the time spent up there is generally compensated with only single-dollar tips. The real money comes from working the floor, so extra time on stage is to be avoided at all costs.

More serious infractions are fined: $25 if your stockings have a run, $50 for lateness, $100 for missing a night of work regardless of the reason, $500 for missing work on a holiday, like Christmas Eve. Payment is exacted for absences without exception. Illnesses, a death in the family, emergencies of any kind cut no ice with the management. In this respect, the job is like the military. There is only one acceptable response after going AWOL: *No excuse, sir, there is no excuse.*

As a result, dancers drag themselves to work even when they're very sick. Recently I worked with the flu. My throat was sore, my voice nearly gone. To be heard at the club you have to shout above the music, and since I didn't want to do that, I had an inspiration: I would pretend to be mute. All night I indicated with hand signals, to men I hadn't met before, that I couldn't speak. Afterward, when I got home, I realized I'd made more money than ever before.

The Catwalk is a place where I can go up to a man I've never seen or spoken to, take his face in my hands, and say, "How beautiful you are." It's a place one can touch and be touched. There is an easy physical intimacy between strangers, an immediacy to each encounter. I trace scars, asking, "What happened here?" I smooth hair back from foreheads and loosen ties. I knead muscles, telling every single customer: "You work too hard."

"I know," they respond, to a man.

The strip joint is supposed to be about fantasy, but sometimes it seems to be about the bare bones of reality. The veil that hangs between the sexes on the outside—the guarded gaze, the pretended disinterest—is lifted; the men in their naked desire often seem more exposed than the women. Once I was in conversation with a customer whose friends were impatient to leave. We were seated at a table and his companions kept glancing pointedly at their watches. He ignored them. Finally one of them tugged at his sleeve.

"Tom, come on, look at the time. We gotta *go*, man."

He barely looked up. "Go ahead without me."

"What! You're not coming? You can't be serious."

Finally he turned to his friend with an incredulous glare, as if he couldn't believe he was being interrupted. "Come on, man, what's with you? *Can't you see I'm talking to a female?*"

I was on the side stage the other night—a little caged-in platform by the bar—when a kid of about twenty-five came up to me.

"Do you remember me?" he asked. "It's Frank, from The Dollhouse."

The Dollhouse was the first place I ever danced. I hadn't seen him in years, since the beginning of my go-go career, and while he did look vaguely familiar, I wouldn't have been able to recall his name.

"Frank!" I said. "Great to see you. It's been a long time! What are you doing these days?"

Sometimes I am still overcome by the surreal nature of such a situation: I am nearly naked, in a cage, striking up casual conversation with a fully clothed boy just beyond the bars.

"I'm a cop now," he told me.

"A cop?"

"Yeah."

"In the N.Y.P.D.?"

"Yeah."

"Really," I said. "Are you packing tonight?"

He nodded, then offered shyly, "Want to feel my gun?"

Of course I did. It was at the small of his back and I reached around and stroked it. It was an arousing moment, seeming as primal, as quintessential a male-female exchange as the rest of what goes on in there. We might have been a small boy and girl in that age-old transaction: "I'll show you mine if . . ."

Just minutes ago, I'd asked a guy in a cowboy hat, "Are you a cowboy?"

"No," he answered.

"An outlaw?"

He shook his head.

"What then?"

"A photographer," he told me.

"Well, I was warm," I said. "Think about it: a cowboy, an outlaw, and a photographer. What do all of you have in common? You all shoot!"

He answered, "I think all men have that in common."

He was much cleverer than I was, and he wasn't even trying.

I'd rather strip than waitress, or temp, or work as a receptionist. I've done all of the above and found them equally degrading, far less lucrative, and not nearly as interesting. Stripping brings me into contact with women and men from all walks of life. Some of the dancers are single mothers. Some are putting themselves through school or pursuing an artistic career. Others are just indulging expensive habits and a few are hustlers and junkies. The men are equally diverse. Stockbrokers come in and so do construction workers. There are the stereotypical dirty old men, and there are fresh-faced boys in for bachelor parties. I have dozens of conversations a night. It is unusual for an hour to go by in which I don't learn something new.

The stage names the girls choose for themselves have such fire and color, such a poignant and hopeful poetry: *Ambrosia. Blaze. Clementine. Delicia. Electra. Fantasia. Gypsy. Harlowe. Isis. Jade. Keiko. Lolita. Magdalene. Nikki. Odessa. Precious. Queenie. Ruby. Sapphire. Tabitha. Una. Vixen. Wanda. Xiola. Yasmine. Zora.*

Elissa Wald

*

The job allows me to wear costumes and accoutrements I would seldom have a chance to indulge in otherwise: elbow-length gloves, thigh-high boots, feather boas, sequins, long velvet gowns that lace up the front. It is the stuff of old-time movies, of vaudeville. I even went through a phase where I wore a pair of angel's wings.

I dress like a sanitation worker much of the time when I'm not at work. I go out in shapeless, oversized clothing, hair pulled back into a slovenly knot, little or no makeup. Part of it is exhaustion, the desire to be comfortable and warm after so many hours in spiked heels and a thong. Part of it is wanting a respite from male appraisal.

I like dancing for the customers most of the other girls are afraid to approach: dwarves, amputees, men in wheelchairs. When they come into the club, I'm across the room like a shot. Once I danced for a guy with a very unfortunate birthmark: a dark splotch, almost perfectly round, directly in the middle of his face like a bull's eye. To me, he automatically had an edge on everyone else, the power that would come from walking around thus marked all his life. He had endured and by now, I could only assume, had the strength and stamina only such a person could possess. I wanted to rub up against him, in the hope that some of it would rub off on me.

The girls take care of each other. An outsider might imagine that the strip joint is an atmosphere that fosters competition, jealousy, backstabbing. But every dancer I've encountered seems to share the conviction that it's Us against Them. It's a tight sisterhood, and all of us call the house-mother—the woman who oversees the dressing room, who provides aspirin and tampons and will fix a torn piece of clothing in a pinch—"Mom."

The other night while I was on stage, I had some words with a customer. He took a deep drag on his cigarette and blew the smoke directly in my face. I countered by spitting into his. The roar that went up from the sidelines was like the sound in a stadium when the home team scores. All the girls in the house, it seemed, had erupted in savage joy: "Yeah, Jo-Jo! You go, girl!" My immediate rush of pleasure was soon replaced by fear as I waited for him to report me to the management. He left instead, slunk out the door, and I realized it was the reaction of the girls that had most likely saved me. He must have perceived the atmosphere as too hostile to stay another minute.

Another illustration: one recent night after work there were no cabs outside the club. I began trudging toward the nearest avenue—Ninth— but when I got there no cars were in sight. It was 4:15 in the morning, sleet was coming down hard, and I was alone in the middle of midtown with all that money. Somewhat anxious now, I began straining for a lit storefront, an open bodega to wait by, when a cab came around the corner and stopped. The back door opened and a female voice summoned me from the interior. "Jo-Jo! What are you doing out here alone? Get in!"

I approached the car and saw Serena, one of the other dancers, in the backseat. "Oh, Serena, hi," I said. I was slightly bewildered. "I live down on Avenue D, do we . . . do we live in the same direction?"

"It doesn't matter," she said. "Just get in."

One night I was dancing for a guy right next to the stage, and the girl who was on it leaned toward me. We kissed wordlessly above the man's head, as if by some prearranged choreography. I'd never seen her before, didn't know even her stage name; in fact, I still don't.

When you're out in the daytime and you see another dancer on the street, you don't always acknowledge each other. Your eyes will meet, and often there will be an almost imperceptible shake of the head, an indication that you shouldn't approach. Maybe she's with family, or a guy who doesn't know what she does. And even if she can think fast enough to in- vent another context for knowing you, the two of you probably don't know each other's real names. You don't want to unthinkingly say, "Hey, Bambi," or "Amber" or "Gemini" or "Venus." So it's best to not even speak to each other; you'll see her later, maybe even tonight. Still, there's an ex- citement in this silent communiqué, a sense of two spies exchanging sig- nals in enemy territory.

A variation on this theme takes place when the Gaiety boys come into the club. The Gaiety is a gay male strip bar just a block and a half away, and a lot of the male dancers there are straight. They come to The

Catwalk between their own stage sets as an antidote to the predatory male energy directed at them all night. The Gaiety boys are as good as it gets, as far as Catwalk clientele: they're clean, smooth, gorgeous, muscle-bound, and loaded. The condescension so prevalent in most of the customers is wholly absent in them. Their attitude is: *We know exactly what you're dealing with in here; you are our sisters in slavery; let's just help each other through it in any way we can.* They pay $20 to $50 for a dance. They come back at 4:00 A.M. to take you to breakfast. You compare notes over eggs and toast. They understand every single thing you say.

When I'm not having breakfast with a male counterpart, or any of the other girls, I often go alone. As a rule I don't eat for several hours before work, and then I dance for eight hours straight. At 4:00 A.M. I'm wired and ravenous, and there's an all-night diner around the corner. At that time it's nearly deserted, and arriving there is like walking into an Edward Hopper painting. There is something satisfying in the wan quiet. I have a sense of a lull in the action, of a space between the night's work and the average person's morning. It's an empty pocket and I'm in it, bone-tired and anonymous and cozy. I feel all alone in the world but right now it feels good instead of bad. I scribble notes on the napkins and paper placemats. I order comfort food: a baked potato, a cup of soup.

A customer—I'll call him Al—taught me one of the most important lessons of my life. I'd danced for him several times when he invited me to come to the restaurant he owned, an upscale grill in SoHo. Several weeks later, I did go in there, and while my friend and I waited to be seated, Al walked by several different times. He kept glancing at me with a puzzled expression, as if to say, "I know I've seen you before, but where?" I thought it better not to enlighten him, surrounded as he was by his staff, and the evening passed without a word exchanged between us.

About a week later, he was back in The Catwalk. I went over to him.

"Hey, Al," I said. "I took you up on your invitation and came into the restaurant last week. But I guess you didn't recognize me with clothes on."

"That was *you!*" he exclaimed. "That was driving me crazy, I *knew* I knew you, but for the life of me I couldn't place you."

"Yeah, well, I could see that," I said. "But of course I didn't want to say anything in front of your employees."

"Why not?" he wanted to know.

"Oh," I said, startled. "You mean, it would have been okay?"

"Well, I'm here . . . right?" he said, ". . . so it has to be okay."

Said so simply, yet it struck like lightning, left me open-mouthed in amazement. *I'm doing it, so it has to be all right.* I never lied about my job again.

The manager can walk into the girls' locker room at any time without knocking. The Champagne Lounge host, the D.J., and the janitor have to knock, and will wait outside until everyone is "decent." The half-nakedness outside in the club—exhibited from the stage, revealed by degrees, washed in neon and bared against music—acquires the siren pull of eroticism; whereas our total nudity in the dressing room, under the cheap fluorescent-tube lighting, is no more exciting than the bodies of livestock in a pen.

A scene from my second year in the business:

It was fifteen minutes before the night shift would begin, and there were perhaps two dozen girls in the locker room when Randall, the manager, strode in, dragging Maggie by the upper arm. Maggie worked the middle shift, from 5:00 P.M. till 1:00 in the morning. She was a rail-thin, statuesque blonde, on this evening decidedly glaze-eyed. Randall was in a barely contained rage.

"Maggie, you're gone. Get dressed and get out."

"Randall!" she said wildly. "What did I do?!"

"If you're not out of here of your own accord in exactly ten minutes, I'm throwing your ass in the street, and I don't care if you're butt naked. If you don't believe that, keep trying to talk to me."

Maggie was crying now, her tears mascara-black. She moved, sniffling and unsteady, to her locker and began to get dressed.

Randall addressed the rest of us. "For the information of everyone else, Maggie has just been fired for doing cocaine in this club. You just have to look at her to see she's fucked up. She wasn't fucked up when she got here at five o'clock. But she's fucked up now. What does that mean? It means she's fucking up on my time. In my space!"

Elissa Wald

Maggie tried to cut in. "Randall, I'm —"

"Eight minutes and counting, Maggie." He paused. "You girls have tried my patience to the limit. Every night I reiterate my warnings about the plainclothes pigs crawling all over this place. If you think I'm going to get closed down because of your indiscretion, you'd better think again." He opened the door of the dressing room and called out to George, the janitor. "George! Come in here."

George entered.

"George, the girls are at the nose candy again," Randall told him. "They have to be sniffing their lines in the bathroom, because those are the only closed doors they have to hide behind. So I want you to go get your crowbar and take the bathroom doors off their hinges."

"Yes, sir," George said. He went out again.

There was a stunned silence in the dressing room. Finally Diamond broke it. "The bathroom doors are coming off? Permanently?"

"You heard right."

"Then I'm quitting," she said. "I'm sorry, I can't deal with that."

"Good-bye," Randall said. He looked around. "Anyone else who shares Diamond's point of view is free to check out of this job right now."

"I'm with her," Mercedes said. "This is supposed to be a club, not a prison."

"Nice knowing you," Randall said. "Anyone else?"

Silence.

"The rest of you, be ready to start at eight as usual."

The atmosphere in the dressing room had been altered. There was a general air of resignation and defeat. Above the lowered heads and averted eyes, I met Randall's gaze. I stared at him in a kind of daze and as he stared straight back at me I felt the heat rushing to my face. His recognition of my arousal intensified it, made it almost painful. The music from outside the door seemed to become more audible as we locked eyes.

There were a handful of such moments while Randall was the manager, unsettling moments: the slow burn, some unspeakable exchange that never even attempted to find words, a secret betrayal of my rightful allegiances. Another one came a few weeks later. I was working the room, circulating on the main floor, and as I walked by the leather sofas that line the back wall, a man touched my arm. "You. Are you available for a private dance?"

"Of course I am." I smiled. "I'm Jo-Jo. And you are?"

"Jo-Jo, I'm John. And this," he indicated the kid beside him, a boy of about 18, "is my young friend Ben. I'm kind of showing him the ropes." He winked at me as he took $20 from his wallet and slid it into my garter. "So I'd like you to dance for him."

"John, it would be my pleasure," I said. I moved to the boy, invaded the space between his knees, and began slowly stripping off my dress.

"Touch her," John said to him.

Ben shot his older friend a nervous glance. His hands stayed at his sides.

"Go on," John repeated. "Touch her."

"I thought the guys aren't allowed to touch the dancers," Ben said.

John reached out and ran a possessive hand up my flank. I closed my eyes.

"Look at her," I heard John say. "Is she all upset? Is she yelling for a bouncer?" He caressed me further, moving his hand to the inside of my thigh. I felt my breathing become rapid and shallow.

"See?" John went on. "She wants it. She wants you to touch her. She's a woman, she needs it. Go ahead. Put your hands on her."

Ben tentatively put his hand on my other leg. The two men stroked me simultaneously: John as an owner would stroke a pet, Ben with tremulous disbelief. I shivered in a genuine response. Suddenly Jimmy, the bouncer, materialized. He grabbed John's wrist in his formidable grip. Ben snatched his hand away.

"What the fuck do you think you're doing?" Jimmy growled. He squeezed the other man's wrist in his fist.

"Ah—don't—" John gasped.

"You picked the wrong girl, scumbag. Naw, scratch that; you ain't allowed to touch *any* of the girls. But especially not Randall's girl."

This was the first time I heard someone articulate what I thought was my own private knowledge, the most subtle understanding.

Jimmy gave the man's wrist a vicious twist before releasing it. "Now you got thirty seconds to get the fuck out of here."

Elissa Wald

John and Ben scrambled up and scurried out of the club. I pulled my dress back on, not looking at Jimmy. My face was burning, my body too.

"Jo-Jo," Jimmy said. "Whaddaya doin'? Whaddaya fuckin' *thinkin'*?"

I couldn't look at him.

"Randall wants to talk to you," Jimmy said. "He said to send you to his office."

Randall's office was in the basement. He was behind his desk when I entered. He indicated that I should sit across from him and he passed one hand wearily over his eyes before speaking.

"What are you trying to do, Jo-Jo?" he asked. "I don't believe what I just saw with my own eyes." He paused. "The middle of the floor! *Two* scumbags! Their paws all over you! And you panting and squirming like a bitch in heat."

"I'm sorry, Randall."

"You think this is a jokc? Think I'm playing with you?"

"No..."

"You think I won't fire you?"

I was silent, staring at the cluttered surface of the desk. But I thought, *Yes. Yes, I do think you won't fire me.*

"This is my last warning to you," he said finally. "If you provoke me one more time, you're out of here."

"I won't," I said. "I'm sorry. Thank you."

Did I love Randall? I did love him a little. It pains me to admit this.

Randall was a long time ago. After he left, Richie became the manager, and after Richie it was Johnny, and now it's Anthony. I never felt anything for any of the others. I don't know where Randall is now.

The terrible and redemptive aspects of the business will balance each other out for some time before the whole proposition begins to turn like milk. Sooner or later, for every dancer, the time comes when you can't swallow it anymore. Looking back on all the times I've left, I can't really pinpoint what in particular, if anything, finally made me walk. Maybe it was the sight of Angel, a feverish dancer trying to sleep between stage sets, curled by the locker-room radiator in her pink bikini, lying on the bare linoleum. Maybe it was the man who threw his single dollar bills one by one onto the stage floor, so we would have to bend over to get them.

As for this time around, not long ago I went to work a few hours after putting my cat to sleep. The cat was old and very sick, but I was heartbroken and unable to check my grief at the door.

"Whatsa matter, Jo-Jo," the Champagne Lounge host wanted to know. "Why such a sad face?"

"My cat died this afternoon," I told him.

Incredibly, his doughy face creased into a grin. "Aw look, honey, don't take it too hard," he guffawed. "As long as your other pussy's holding up."

Yes, the job can make you hate men.

"Laying and paying," is a phrase you hear repeated like a mantra in the locker room. "That's all they're good for. Laying. And paying."

As if it's a point of pride that the exploitation is mutual.

Yes, the job can make you hate yourself. Because you're holding up the other half of that transaction, perpetuating it night after night after night of your life.

There are tell-tale signs of when a dancer is on her way out: arriving at work five minutes prior to the beginning of a shift, instead of the half-hour needed to get ready; drinking too early; passing most of the night at the bar; crying on stage. For myself, I know the jig is almost up when I come out of the dressing room and instead of trying to identify the man most likely to spend a lot of money, I look for someone I think I can stand to talk to. This is the wrong attitude.

Last night the ache was upon me and I kept searching for, seizing upon, any man who might alleviate some small part of it. I walked around the club in several desperate circles, scanning the crowd for someone who seemed strong, smart, competent, gentle, kind. There was no one like that anywhere.

Once again, it's almost time to go.

Elissa Wald

Felicia Ward

Good Night Moon

From *Nimrod International Journal*

It's my birthday. I feel ambushed by their stares. Every thought scatters—ricochets from unmade beds to unwashed dishes and back again to my children, one-two-three, kneeling between wall and bed. Their frosting-smeared faces are as obscene to me as a baboon's bright blue ass and just as unexpected.

I keep not hitting them. I keep not hearing crunch of bones; keep not seeing leather shoes welting skin. I look into those familiar eyes, and I want to give in to the way I feel about them. Relent to mothering, the way one finally gives into a virus; adjusting to clogged airways, mucous and phlegm.

I want the fever of memory to break, so we can breathe again.

Last year, as a birthday surprise, my husband arranged for the aunts to take our children, and spirited me away for a long weekend. Ninety minutes after we left our house in Berkeley, we were at my mother-in-law's place. A small house overlooking Austin Creek.

We were on a peace-keeping mission. My husband wanted to save our marriage. For a change, I indulged his every wish. We spent the first morning of a three day weekend sharing the same deck chair, our legs intertwined. I even let Gus play with my hair.

"Honey," he said, "I'm experiencing *déjà vu* all over again."

To humor him, I tilted my head back and planted a dry kiss on his throat. Content, he worked his way over every square inch of my head, oiling my scalp, and twisting my thick dark wool into locks.

"Look," Gus said, pointing up at the sky, "a portent."

The rising sun hit a stand of redwood trees, and turned the bark bone white. A breeze, as gentle as a newborn's breath, agitated the branches. "What's important?" I asked.

"Portent. An omen, a sign."

"I know what portent is, Gus. Don't patronize me."

"I'm not. Honey, look . . . right there . . . all silvery . . . see?"

A clump of clouds gave way, and I could see long silken threads floating across blue sky.

"Baby spiders," I said, disappointed, "ballooning to escape cannibalistic mothers."

"Like in *Charlotte's Web?*"

"Exactly."

I have three children: boy-boy-girl.

I call my oldest son my "prodrome" baby. He's the result of a vulvar tingle; followed by a not unpleasant swelling, that in my case, masqueraded as lust. Members of my husband's latte crowd called Herpes, the "Spanish fly" of the 8os. More potent than oysters and Champagne, it was epidemic among his friends. My husband used to call this explanation my Herpes defense. Whatever. One hundred hours of labor made me a mother, a mama, a mommy, forever.

I breast-fed Ben, blood and milk. Not intentionally. I didn't have a clue how to toughen up my tits; get them ready for a toothless carnivore.

Ask the aunts. That's what Gus said.

I told him no, they're as sterile as mules.

Your doctor then, he said.

Ding-ding-ding, I pretended to clang his head like a bell, to remind him: HMO, remember. They've already pamphleted me to death.

End of conversation.

Our second son is the result of ordinary lust. He loved to suck. My husband, the English professor, preferred I say "suckle." I only wish I could have vacuum-suctioned Miles to his bologna-colored paps.

Now my daughter, Rachel, was a dream. She developed an allergy to her mama's milk. She read my mind. I wish the other two had considered that option.

Fatherhood has always suited Gus. He loves his sons, but he's wild about Rachel. Completely smitten. When other men crowed about their son's perfect little penis, delighted in the first time, undiapered, the little whizzer pumped daddy full in his face with pee, my husband went on and on about his daughter's "internal maternal devices."

"Can you believe it?" he says, to a banquet table full of his academic cronies, "my baby girl's uterus is about the size of a garlic clove. Her ovaries, the same circumference around as a sweet pea."

"You mean a black-eyed pea, don't you?" his department chair says.

All conversation stopped. There was no clink of crystal against dentures. No pink-lipsticked faculty wives, dabbing at the corners of their smiles with white linen napkins. Everyone turned to look at me, nine long noses wrinkling, like they'd discovered a bad smell in the house. The glass of Merlot in my hand tipped, just a millimeter too far, and dribbled wine onto the tablecloth. My husband didn't notice the stain creeping over to his side of the table.

"Right," he says, his blue eyes shining, "just think, she's only four years old and my daughter has all the eggs she'll ever need."

"Thank goodness," his department chair says, winking at his wife.

What I had to do next—the words I used to punctuate every single blow—made that the last meal I ever shared with my untenured husband.

All winter, from December to March, I moved my things from my husband's house to my father's. I didn't want help. I wanted the dumb numbing repetitive motion of punching collapsed cardboard into boxes. The satisfying ache of sore muscles. The physical exhaustion that comes from carrying 57 boxes up and down three flights of stairs.

On the last day of the move, the students I'd hired to haul furniture got lost. I told them to look for the brown shingle house with the stunted "Juliet" balcony, and the orange gingerbread trim.

They pulled up to the front door five minutes later.

When they were gone, I stood at the kitchen sink and watched a weary stream of ants pour through a crack in the kitchen window.

I pinched one dead.

My father would be home soon. "One hard knock," he'd probably say, about the divorce, "that don't make you no tree."

I don't know what that means either. I've spent half my life trying to figure that man out. I was five years old when he sent me to live with his sisters: The Aunts. The first time I saw them, all I could think was, what big eyes they had; what long white teeth. When they couldn't resist planting wet kisses on my cheeks, I asked them why they looked like walnuts and smelled like Spam.

Aunt Sis stayed Aunt Baby's hand; caught it by the wrist in mid-flight. Under her breath, Aunt Baby said, "I ought to slap her to kingdom come."

Aunt Sis said, "Not tonight you don't."

I'll never forgive them for not taking me and my children in.

Right at the breakfast table, with all three of my children looking her straight in the mouth, Aunt Sis says, "You been with us two weeks. You need to go on home, Honey. Your daddy's house can't take nothing away from you it aint already took."

I could hear my spine straightening. The vertebrae clicking into place.

"We'll keep your doggone chirren here with us," Aunt Baby said, " 'til you can get your things moved in. I know your daddy's house is going to be a tight fit, but we old now. You can see that. And mind you, if you hear the rustle of love, you get on back to Russ."

"Gus."

"Gus, go on back to him."

I pinched another ant dead ... then another. I regretted it later. I understood their urgency. But I couldn't stop. I wasn't going to shoot myself. I'm not sure how much time passed before I gave it up. There were just too many, and they had a smell.

*

Felicia Ward

At eight o'clock, my father came in with take-out. Won ton soup. Sweet and sour. Chow mein with crispy noodles. My favorites, he reminded me.

I couldn't eat. I did crack open my fortune cookie. It read, "You have a good sense of humor." I guess I do. For the first time in 30 years I spent the night in my father's house.

I slept like the dead.

Saturday morning, I woke to cold winter light. A quiet house, empty of children. My father said he'd bring them here, around seven o'clock, along with two birthday cakes. Chocolate for me. Lemon cake, with Cookie-Monster-blue frosting for Rachel.

I forced myself out of bed to do the routine. Pee. Wash. Check out the face for changes. Pillow tracks, as deep as tribal markings, criss-crossed both cheeks. I looked soft and rumpled. Nothing like myself. I got back in bed.

By noon, I was as numb as a rock from too much sleep.

By two o'clock I was as lonely as God on the fifth day; before he created Adam; before Eve was a twinkle in his eye.

By three, I needed my children's sounds. In this house, I can't be a mother without them.

I couldn't face unpacking, so I wandered from room to room trying out chairs; opening and closing cupboards; and nibbling from a tube of raw cookie dough I found in the fridge. I saved rifling through my father's bedroom closets for last. I didn't find a thing. No letters in his 50-year-old chiffarobe. No newspaper clippings in a shoe box. No death certificates under the mattress.

There was one photograph. Me and the X. A mall pose excreting matrimonial bliss. I turned it face down and walked back to the living room.

The best thing about this house is the view. Sitting at the living room window you get water, hills, sky and block after block of one- and two-story houses marching down to the San Francisco Bay.

Getting this house was the equivalent of winning the lottery for my parents. Nate and Nola Choyce were part of the great migration north, from Louisiana and Texas, in the 40s. Him a longshoreman at the naval shipyards; her a cook at the university. Colored people living in high cotton. They should have had it made. They were the reason I could sit there, and watch the darkening sky.

Winter sunsets here, are rudely beautiful. Shameless. At five o'clock the sun collapsed into the bay, leaving deep violet hills, aqua blue water, and clouds as outrageously pink as the G-string on a drag queen. Three minutes, and it was over—everything faded to black.

I left the window to turn on a lamp.

When I came back, I could see the glow of street lights, and my face mirrored in the glass. I don't know why I look like I do. My X used to say that no matter how angry I got, I always managed to look serene. The aunts swear I look like a dark skinned Jackie-O. They don't say pre-Onassis, but post grim tragedy. They do say I have her same wide set eyes. Ditto, the Mona Lisa smile. The dark clothes. They don't mention the secrets either. That's our primary kinship. I should be stark raving mad. I'm not.

I'm a 34-year-old black woman, alive at the end of the 20th century and passing for sane. Believe me, that's saying something. I am not one to fall apart. I heard my father say that to one of the detectives, 30 years ago. He said, "My little girl, Honey, she's not going to fall apart."

And I'm not.

I understand the colored tradition of preferring truth over facts. I have a completely unsentimental view of what happened in this house. Aunt Baby and Aunt Sis painted very particular and peculiar pictures of our family history.

Aunt Baby's the one who told me, "Your mama's heart was as numb as a foot in a too-tight shoe."

Aunt Sis backed her up, saying, "I believe it was her raisin-hearted ways that led her to stray."

"Your mama had everything going for her," Aunt Baby said, "she was as pretty as Dorothy Dandridge, as smart as Eleanor Roosevelt—"

"She had feet like Harriet Tubman," Aunt Sis said, "hard and callused, not at all tender."

They didn't mention my mother's daughters. I learned to steel myself against feeling anything for them. What happened is neither here nor there. As my father would say, "There are worse things than losing your mother."

Now, I'll be the first one to *Amen!* that, because, it's being a mother that stains my linen. My children smell like the spare change my father used to keep in his pockets. The warm penny he doled out every day.

That's how my children smell when they've been playing outside all day—like warm, copper pennies. And if they stand too close, if I get that smell, it brings back the sound of my mother tearing rags to stuff in the windows. Then the whole day long that's all I get, the sound of tearing— and I can't shake it, unless I sleep—and when I sleep I get one dream: *It's March 15, 1965. My fifth birthday. I'm in the big bed I share with my sisters. I wake up first. When I open my eyes, there's a red-and-white dress floating above my head, hiding my mother's face. She's standing over me twisting the dress back and forth in the early morning light, admiring it, checking and re-checking the seams for loose threads, the buttons, the lace trim. It's perfect. White organdy with a red-checked apron. There are tiny red polka dots on the puffy sleeves, and the hem is a waterfall of flounces.*

I am a big girl. Smart.

I don't believe her when she says we're going back to Texas.

That's the only dream I ever dream. It's easy enough to manage if I can keep a little distance, a cushion of air, between me and my children. It's not like they need lap time anymore. Not even Rachel. I tell you, my daughter's a dream.

I understand why my folks chose California. There were all these things not to be afraid of. Tornadoes. Hurricanes. Rednecks. Not where you could see them. I love raising my kids here. My children are safe from just about everything and everyone but me. That's something I can't ever guarantee. My mother ended it all, for herself and three daughters. In one fell swoop—whoosh—they were gone.

Why?

I don't have the be-all, end-all answer to that, but I do keep a running list. I started it when I became a mother. I've listed "forks in the trash can" at least 17 times.

Last night after dinner, I fished two forks out of the trash can; dunked them in the dishwater; and towel dried my hands. I didn't hurry. I put the leftovers away and tied up the trash. Then I left the kitchen for the living room. I could hear the television, and the sound of my father snoring. I didn't rush. Before I reached my children, I wanted to let my breathing return to normal. That takes time. It's not like I've mastered the "three maternal powers." That's what the X and I called them. It was a game we played. He understood my history.

When I got to the living room, I waited in the doorway. I could see my father sprawled in front of the television, the fingers of both hands tucked inside the waistband of his trousers. He's like me. Sleeps like the dead. It would take dynamite to rouse him. The aunts say we're both lucky to be alive. I've never been able to decide whether that's a curse or a blessing.

Rachel was using her granddad as a headrest. Our Siamese cat, my share of the community property, leg gracefully extended was licking his pedigree. Ben and Miles were in a tug-of-war over a bag of chips. I didn't try to stop them. I wanted to see who'd win, who's stronger. It wasn't much of a contest. Ben gave in first. I still didn't say a word. I wanted them to sense my presence on their own. That's maternal power number one.

The living room was smothered with furniture. Three coffee tables stacked waist high. Two side chairs. My father's 30-year-old Barcalounger, permanently stuck in recline. Two couches, one mossy green, and one gold. I couldn't even see my mother's piano, for the nubby orange love seat propped against the wall.

The sight of my life squeezed inside that room deflated every power I even thought I had. The kids didn't notice me at all. Before I could regain my full strength, Rachel, savoring momentary possession of the remote control, flipped through every channel twice. "The Simpsons" flashed on and off. "Seinfeld." Moesha on the WB—then back to Bart. When I saw Ben's head begin to pull in my direction, I made my words sting, like a wet towel on naked skin.

"Get to bed," I said, "Now!"

They were not impressed.

The boys whined in unison. Drawn out grating phantom-of-the-opera chords. All the organ keys flattened at once. Pathetic and miserable. "Ma-a-a," my Ben says, "our shows aint off yet."

Felicia Ward

"You see this?" I took a deep breath before I held up a fork and added, "Guess where I found it?"

Rachel's head swiveled back and forth searching my face first, then Ben's. Her old woman's eyes taking everything in. I could feel the second power surging through me. The power to make them obey. The hairs on the back of my neck were standing on end.

The boys got up from the floor, mouths zipped shut, eyes focused on the floor. Rachel, on the other hand, decided to rub the cat; long hard strokes in the wrong direction. Anyone but a four-year-old could tell by the eye the cat had shut, and the other eye it had half-opened, that any minute, it was going to rip her to shreds. I reached over and pushed the thing off her lap. It curled itself around my legs, complaining in that eerie human-child sounding yeowl that only Siamese cats have.

I took the remote control away from Rachel, and aimed it at the TV. That's when Miles said, "Don't turn it off ma, it'll make you sad."

That completely broke the spell. I tried to cover by pointing down the hall. Both boys slunk out of the room. Apparently, they hadn't noticed the depletion of my powers. On the other hand, baby sister made me usher her out, with a swat on her behind. Clear evidence my powers had evaporated.

Rachel took her own sweet time, back pressed against the wall, to slide down the entire length of the hallway, scooting inch by inch, just as slowly as she could possibly make herself go.

She stopped at the open bedroom door and demanded, "Lights!"

I flicked them on, and used the third maternal power. I resisted the urge to kick her into the room. Instead, I distracted myself with petroleum based toddler detritus. It was scattered from one end of the room we shared to the other. I picked up Pocohantas Barbie by the head, Little Mermaid Barbie by the leg, and I kicked Tickle-Me-Elmo to my daughter's side of the room.

Rachel ignored me, until she heard Tickle-Me-Elmo giggling. Then she shucked off her slippers with tight little kicks, straight into the air. She barely missed my face. Luckily for both of us, she chose that moment to transform herself into a frog. She hopped the rest of the way to her bed, and landed with her tail end pointed up at me. I lifted the covers so she could get underneath. Then I said, "Kiss mommy good night."

"No kiss," she said, "Story."

I was relieved. I didn't want to touch her. How many times, I wondered, did it take before a mother gave in and pushed a pillow over that dimpled face. I made a mental note to add slipper kicking to my list.

Just then, rapid-fire belching erupted from the boys room—followed by muffled laughter. "Choose a book," I said, holding up one finger, "I'll be right back."

Standing outside my old bedroom door, I stopped. I'm not one for surprises, not really. I coughed to signal, "Mommy's coming."

Unfortunately, when I opened the door, I forgot my own strength, let it get away from me. The damned thing swung open and kept on going. I didn't want to, but I looked. When I pulled the door back, a new layer of plaster crumbled to the floor. Where knob meets wall a huge receptive hole, about the size of a newborn baby's head, was at least two inches deeper.

My father. He refuses to make any changes in this house. He will not paint. He won't remove my mother's 26 pillbox hats, or her sherbet colored suits. Nada. Nothing. Not even a $1.99 door stop.

I turned around to face my boys. They were too frightened to blink. I stared right back. I didn't apologize. It was late. I abandoned the maternal powers for fast, mean "mamalese."

"Lie down. Shut up. Go to sleep."

They obeyed. I tucked blankets under chins, took a deep breath and planted kisses near cheeks. The folds of Miles' neck smelled like warm pennies. I studied his face. He's my link to the maternal line. The aunts say my children are watered down. Too much white blood they say. I don't know about that, but Miles has my mother's eyes. Her fuzzy, soft around the hairline, nappy in the back, brick red hair. Her fawn-colored skin. He's not dark like me.

Love will obliterate him.

That's what I think when I see him laying there with his thumb inside his mouth. The little finger of the same hand feathering the tip of his nose. Every nerve ending reduced to this single pleasure. "It's mommy," his mouth full of thumb reassures. Pathetic.

I walked to the door and heard rustling. When I turned around, Ben had raised himself up on one elbow to blow me a kiss. I shot him one

Felicia Ward

back, and he smiled. I pitched my voice low to say, "Don't make me come back in here."

Miles paused mid-suck. The sappy smile on Ben's face disappeared.

I closed the door behind me, thinking, I don't care what anybody says. By the time I was seven years old, I already knew about the poorhouse, atomic bombs, assassinations, napalm, polio, the Klan. I'd seen Buddhist monks go up in flames. I understood the need to self immolate. I'd seen those little Texas girls, cotton wadded in blinded eyes. I understood that some folks' anger was explosive. Others had hate that seared to the bone. And of course, I had my own mother. I wanted my children to know fear.

Fear couldn't hurt them. In fact, they might need it some day.

Walking back down the hall, my naked feet on hardwood floors made a heavy slapping sound. The same sound my mother's feet made, when she went room to room collecting daughters. By the time I reached Rachel, I had a briny taste in my mouth.

Baby sister was wide awake, a thin book clutched in her hands. A gift from my imagination-stunted mother-in-law. She's responsible for all the Birkenstocked-parent approved, dull as water, culturally appropriate pulp, masquerading as children's literature my daughter owns.

I try to balance the Disney-Barney-Blue Dog palaver she rains on my children with fairy tales. The Brothers Grimm. Hans Christen Anderson. Ice Queens. Bloody red shoes. The possibility of being baked and eaten alive. The classics. I'd place Grimm in every home, like the Gideons do with the Bible.

The last hours of my childhood: the sirens; the breaking glass; my sister's faces; and my mother's as dull as unfired clay—they'll always be what they were. That's something I can't ever change. But fairy tales were my trail of bread crumbs. My way out of the forest. I will always thank my mother for that. There was no other savior in this house.

My boys may have already chosen the weakest of survival weapons. Ben wants to please others. Miles (according to the aunts) was weaned too soon. But I think, maybe, Rachel has a chance. My youngest child is a lot like me. She plays hide and seek as if it was a war game, as if her life depended on it.

I perched on the edge of Rachel's bed and pretended to read the words printed in her new book. I didn't get very far before she stopped me.

"Mommy," she said, her right eyebrow cocked, "what's oncetupon?"

"Everything that came before right now," I say.

My answer seemed to satisfy her, so I read on, hiding witches and trolls in that story-book bunny's darkening room, until I heard soft breathing.

It's our birthday. I wake to laughter floating through the house. Rachel's bed is empty. Good. Her Grandpa Nate must have banana pancakes on the griddle. I lay there with closed eyes and listen. From the sound of their laugher, my children are drunk on the Sunday sweetness of doing nothing. I swing both feet out of bed and the soft nappy body of Elmo giggles.

I place my full weight on him, but he won't stop. My children do. Their sounds are abruptly cut off, like someone has hands over their mouths. I shove Elmo under my pillow, to shut him up; and my children's sounds start to rise and fall again. I bounce up-and-down on the bed, to make it creak, and their sounds die down completely.

There's no use putting it off. I shrug on my robe, and search for them.

It doesn't take long to find them. They're in the living room, all three sitting in a tight circle, painting each other's faces blue with frosting. When I step inside the room they scatter.

Miles crawls over to the orange love seat on all fours, and slips behind it.

Ben wedges himself underneath the coffee tables.

Rachel thinks we're playing a game. She tags my leg, and calls out, "You're it!" before she scoots under the extended footrest of the Barcalounger. When I see her tuck herself into a tight ball, so that she is hidden in the cavity of my father's chair, my hiding place, I hiss, "What-the-hell-are-you doing?"

My rage is biblical.

I reach down and pull Rachel out by both feet. I drag her over to Miles' hiding place; and yank him out by the arm. Then I haul them both to the center of the room. I get close enough to the stacked coffee tables, to hold Ben down with my foot.

Felicia Ward

"Answer me," I say, measuring each breath, "what-the-hell-are-you-doing?"

Everything is ceremonially quiet.

I don't hear any screams. There is no crying.

I can't tell if they are mute with fear, or if I am deaf with rage.

"Wait here," I say, "don't move an inch."

I leave them to rummage through my still packed boxes, but I can't find what I need. I check the hall closet. My father has cleared it out to make room for us. I try the kitchen: drawers; under the sink; inside the broom closet. I walk back to the living room with the extension cord dangling from my hand.

No children.

Only Puss n' Boots, with frosting-spackled whiskers.

I restrain myself. I don't kick him to kingdom come.

The door to the boys' room is closed.

I put my ear against it and listen.

When I can only hear myself breathing, I turn the knob.

The door swings open with a whoosh of air. I hold on to it this time, and don't let go until the knob is nesting in that hole like a baby in its cradle.

My children are huddled together. Miles is shivering like he's cold. Ben has the hiccups. Rachel has her thumb in her mouth.

I keep the three of them in my line of sight and sneak a look down at my hands. There's no streak of red beneath my nails. No crimped skin. The uncoiled extension cord is limp.

I look at my feet. There's no sign that the earth spins beneath me.

I look back up at my children's fear-struck faces.

There is no evidence that I will ever learn what part of my nature to temper.

My Suburb: Ridgewood, N.J.

From *The New York Times Magazine*

I admit to you, it's sort of a monster. Made completely of 10-gauge stainless steel, inside and out—grill head, cart, sidebar shelves that a set of chubby twins could sit on. Beneath the cover, I've got a porcelain-mesh infrared rotisserie and two heavyweight cast-iron burners that blow 50,000 B.T.U.'s. Oh yes, this is a gas machine. On a hot July night with the knobs maxxed out I think I can almost reach fission. Some grill, you say. Though you, of course, believe in the flavor of charcoal, you believe in the ancient rites of the fire, you believe in the waiting and the sometime heartbreak and you believe in nature and the fates. All this is mature, and good. But out here, on the wide, rectangular pad of my driveway, on the knife edge of these taintless streets, I favor the dream of mastery. I like rolling my grill to the cool of the grass, as far out as the orange extension cord will run, which snakes from inside the garage to the plug end of the rotisserie motor. I like having a couple of trussed chickens fixed on the spit, their skins paprika-rubbed and lumpy beneath with garlic cloves and veins of rosemary. I like reaching underneath and releasing the valve of the propane tank—I've got another in the shed, full and ready, because you run out only when you're grilling—and then flipping the spark igniter, which never works the first time or the second and so makes you cringe, anticipating the basso whoomp of the burn. I like waiting there, nearby, however long, taking an 8-iron to the patches of crab grass, gathering the overripe tomatoes, sipping my near-frozen-cold can of Old Milwaukee, until Michelle calls out from the side door, Are we ready? And I lift the cover, the birds crackling and the barrage of smoke sweet enough to breathe, breathe in deep, though I can't, and I can only whisper, Oh yeah we're ready, we're ready.

I s h l e   P a r k

Ode to Sesshu

From *The Asian Pacific Journal*

Poison bum breeze wafting from the corner seat   eyelids crusted in
    green sleep
but we sit tired enough to stand it.   The chunky Mexican who
    eyed me on the platform
now stands dick-in-my-face in this half vacant car,
glazing me with half vacant eyes
while it pulses sideways in light denim

the floor is a dance of muddy footprints

I do a slow profile of the row rumbling across from me

feet	Nikes	worn leather	gold plastic
legs	jeans	black pants	embroidered lace light filmy gold
			with orange on the trim, an
			open eyelid to the floor
eyes	bloodshot	closed	downcast
head	capped	thin	bunned

the transfer is a mob of shoes, elbows, palms pushing strange backs.

9:45
wrong time frozen on the platform clock

furious beast in black liner,
enraged by the sight of an olive brown
palm at the small of my back
she holds her crotch and calls my man a sellout
vietnam VIETNAM   she spits from toast-of-new-york stained lips

in my dreams I flatten and square her face into a bloody Cubist sculpture
with chunky three inch heels

But Christmas wine spills over rock
Five dollar fruit basket kicked to rails
Torn cover sheet of my discarded book lies
And the flight of green crystal is magic   glitter   dazzling
before it cuts my eye

My boyfriend coaxes me from the tunnel
its mouth as open as any grave
blackness brilliant and smelling deep
the rumble of approaching wind.

being double jointed, I listen to the roll and click of bones at night,
    vaguely waiting for the first real crack.

Francisco Goldman

Mexico DF

From *Gatopardo*

Supposedly, I live in New York City, where, of course, I pay an exorbitant rent for a too small apartment. It can be pretty dispiriting to be stuck inside a small apartment, trying to begin a novel which doesn't want to begin. It is also somewhat incredible that someone like me, who has a hard time sitting still, and does not especially like being alone all day, day after day after day, should have chosen this manner of earning a living.

In New York City late last winter I began a new novel, which, for me at least, can be a tortuous process of writing the same first page over and over for months while waiting for the story I've made-up to finally begin to breathe on its own. New York is a bustling, muscular, exhausting, super-materialistic, brutally expensive workaholic's city where it can often seem that everyone else is enormously wealthy and successful— everyone but yourself and the millions of poor people you pass every day out on the streets and in the subways—where everyone works hard by day and plays hard at night, greedily enjoying the fantastic fruits of their labors. And there you are, still stuck on page one of your novel two months later, and every time you go outside, instead of feeling that you are being followed by Cupid with his bow and arrow, or by any tailwind of providential fortune, there is instead a giant magnet trailing you everywhere you go, pulling money from your pockets. New York can chop you up, when things are not going well, when you are feeling eternally stuck on page one of your novel. And because New York can seem to be such a draining, bullying, overwhelming place, people tend to blame the city itself, rather than themselves, for their problems, blame the city for their loneliness, for their exhaustion, for their frustration, for the violence done to their own nerves, for their own darkness, for their addiction, for whatever ails them, and at times like that, they often dream of escaping to someplace far away—to the mountains, the ocean, the islands, the health spa in the desert, to whatever foreign place their grandparents or parents were born in, to the West Coast. And I am one of the lucky ones, because I actually have a place to escape to. A country house, a hermit's retreat, so to speak. Except my "country house" happens to be in the middle of one of the largest, most polluted, most indisputably corrupt, most incomprehensible cities on earth. My country house is the vast, roomy, practically unfurnished apartment I have rented for the last four years now, for a fifth of what my New York apartment costs me, in La Colonia Condesa, in Mexico's Distrito Federal.

Last April I packed a suitcase and several thousand versions of page one of my novel, and took off, fleeing New York for Mexico, and apart from the occasional quick trip back to NYC, I've been here since. As for the pinche book: one night soon after arriving I went to a party at the writer Mario Bellatín's house, where they ran out of liquor, except that some genius then mixed a sort of pseudo-daiquiri with ice from an obscure source or God knows what, but within minutes of drinking it, I felt something like a mule kick in my entrails, and I went home, and spent the next 48 hours with a hallucination-filled dysenteric fever, during which at some point I dreamed the entire first chapter of my novel, which takes place in a nun's convent a hundred years ago, as if it were something I was living through myself, and I staggered out of bed, transcribed it as well as I could, went back to sleep, dreamed another scene, etceteras, and woke up the next morning almost disappointed to find myself restored to good health. And so, yes, book's been coming along ever since....

*

I've been making Mexico City my second home, off and on, for eight years now. I was probably conceived here: my parents were to have been married in Guatemala City, but at the last minute Archbishop Rossel (then busily conspiring with the CIA in the preparations for the 1954 coup) ruled that my mamita could not marry a Jew in any church under his divine jurisdiction, and so my parents and my mother's family came north to Mexico City, where they were married in a side-chapel of the Metropolitan Cathedral, with rented bridesmaids who, despite the fact that they were on the job, treated the wedding party with that mixture of good-natured hospitality, generosity and elegance for which Mexicans are justly renowned (Borges compared Mexico to a country of tourist guides). My mother still remembers those bridesmaids as if they had been true lifelong friends, and who knows, perhaps they were the happy graces who presided over my conception that very night.

I spent much of the 1980s living in Central America, working as a journalist while trying to become a fiction writer as well, basing myself sometimes out of an empty apartment on the roof of the house where my late abuelos had lived (my newlywed cousins now lived downstairs.) I wrote cronicas and reportajes for magazines, and though these paid modestly, two or three pieces a year was usually all I needed to produce in order to live. But it was impossible, back then, for my magazine to pay me in Guatemala; I had to come north to Mexico City, where the money could be wired to a bank.

In 1983, after a very bad, scary time in Guatemala, a friend and I, another journalist, drove together to Mexico City (never forget finally crossing the border, and the fear and tension draining from our limbs as we shouted curses—which I'm sure they couldn't hear—at the soldiers on the Guatemalan side of the river, and drinking my first delicious Mexican beer, ice-cold). When we reached Mexico City, it was Christmas week, and the bank I had to go to was closed. It seemed—I don't remember clearly—that the bank was going to be closed for the next nine days or so. And I was almost out of money. I stayed in a little hotel in El Centro that

smelled of boiled cauliflower and vinegar. At the hotel desk, they confiscated my passport in lieu of payment.

In the evenings, I'd walk to the Alameda, pay out some of the few pesos I
had left for some tacos. I was impressed by the amazing profusion of
Christmas gifts various governmental ministries and agencies showered
on the journalists I knew who were based here! One night acquaintances
took me to a party sponsored by the Russian Embassy, where we were
nearly drowned in vodka while KGB agents circulated, picking our
brains for info and insight into the situation in Central America. There
was a beautiful prostitute staying on the same floor of my hotel, about
fifteen years older than I, an Anita Ekberg–type, whose florid perfume
perpetually penetrated my room like a delicious cake slowly baking next
door. One lonely Christmas weeknight she struck up a friendly conversation with me that soon turned to business, I had no money, but I did have
this transistor short-wave radio . . .

I lived here all of 1993—renting a room with my girlfriend in the
"Xanadu"-like house that had belonged to El Indio Fernandez—the most
gothic and strange place I've ever lived, but that's a story of its own—and
following our break-up in 1995, I moved here again, devastated, and not
knowing where else to go. In fact, my doctor even advised against it, because I'd somehow developed asthma the year before in Guatemala City,
while doing research in damp, musty archives during a month of 28
straight days of rain, and the mould and hongos and dust of century old
manuscripts and newspapers had somehow infected my lungs. Anyway,
the doctor said, You can't go and live in Mexico City! The pollution . . . !
Your lungs . . . ! And you know what? The Mexico City air cured me! It
somehow scoured my lungs like an industrial cleaner, killed off those
hongo-infected nerve-endings—I haven't had a single attack since. That
year of "starting over" I first rented a tiny rooftop apartment in the Condesa, on Juan Escutia, and there, I began to cure myself of loss, playing
James Brown over and over on my tape player every night, drinking tequila, dancing on the roof like a man both possessed and at least ten years
younger, howling at the moon . . .

*

I have no trouble admitting that I love Mexico City, this city of fantastic negatives—pollution, crime, urban sprawl and ugliness, in-your-face poverty—which exerts such an irresistible, charismatic pull on myself and so many others. Over the last eight years I have lived here with companions and without, while in relationships and during periods of searing loneliness and disappointment; I have finished one novel here, started another (which I eventually finished in NYC) and am now immersed in a third; I have been violently mugged and robbed three times, including one pistol-point kidnapping in a cab, and a savage fight for my life—I do not exaggerate—with two intruders inside the apartment I was renting at the time; I have fallen in love, out of love, and made one mortal enemy, a relationship which, I've learned, demands a nearly similar fidelity and tentativeness as a prospering love does; in other words I have lived here in good times and bad, and yet during the bad times, I am never remotely tempted to blame Mexico City for my problems, in fact I always carry the secret conviction that things would be even worse were I someplace else.

Especially after I've been away for a long time, I love arriving at Mexico Airport, smelling the chemical air, feeling that weighty closeness of the sky, its dirty aluminum flatness, getting stuck in traffic in the taxi, marveling at the rust-streaked concrete ugliness of the buildings all around, their vast repetition, and finding them beautiful. And feeling nervous already about arriving at my apartment, wondering if it will have been broken into again, nervous about having to turn on the gas—if the fixtures or tank haven't been stolen off the roof again—and anticipating already how easy it's going to be to re-establish my routine, my daily rounds of breakfast there, delicious tacos de olla here, lunch there, all within a long work day, capped with drinks at a cantina, almost always El Centenario, with friends, or alone with a book.

I don't claim to know much about Mexico. I don't claim to know the city, the country, even the people, well at all. Though of course a sense of a people is something you inevitably pick up, through your ears, through your skin almost. When people ask me what it is that keeps drawing me

Francisco Goldman

back to Mexico, I usually stammer out some response about the friends I've made, as if in a city of such overwhelming scale, only these most intimate connections are tangible. (It's true though, friends from all over, Cuba, Colombia, Centroamerica, Ireland, Spain, and of course Mexico, and, confusingly, since I don't pretend there's a reason for it, not one from the United States.) But what brings me back here over and over is that sense of everyday routine. By which I mean a sense of how time passes, or can be passed here.

A sense of how people live in Time here, so much differently than how they do in New York. There's much to say about this. It must be one of the great Mexican subjects or themes. Aztec time layered through post-modern Western megalopolis time, and so on. Less pompously, the days seem very long. Long workdays, long lunches, long siestas, long tardes, very long nights. Only the hot water in my apartment is defined by brevity. My days in La Condesa last twice as long as days in New York. I get twice as much done. By refusing to partake of long Mexican lunches with friends and putting off my socializing until the late evening when everyone else is finally getting out of work, I can make one work day feel like two. I perambulate around the Condesa, a neighborhood everyone makes fun but that many want to live in. I don't care, there are trees, a park, a bookstore with pretty and helpful muchachas working in it, and another fantastic second-hand bookstore, and Chuchu my barber who has been cutting hair on that corner for forty years, everything I need is at hand, and I resolutely try to avoid having to go anywhere else in the city until the night or on Sundays, when the avenues and expressways aren't so jammed, and a trip to another neighborhood—because they are all so different in character, and so defined, and sometimes so hidden—feels like a trip to another country. Everyone complains about all the silly trendy imitate–New York kinds of places mushrooming in la Condesa, and the horrible pasta restaurants, and the trendy fresa-this or fresa-that, but I don't care, I pretty much stay out of those places, and begin to forget they're even there: why would I come to Mexico to hang around in a place that feels like its trying to recreate 80s New York at its most fashion-victim-desperate?

*

Of course there's plenty to detest about Mexico City, as there is about any other place: the iron-clad race-based class system here which so many seem to be in denial about; the way everyone goes on about how this person or that person or that place is so horribly fresa while pretending that they themselves aren't as fresa as everyone else, because let's face it, whether it be La Condesa, Coyoacan, Las Lomas, Polanco, San Angel, all of these places and almost all the people in them are essentially fresa— tambien yo!—and people should probably stop pretending that isn't so unless they truly mean to do something about it; anti-Semitism often expressed with a shocking combination of unapologetic vulgarity, ignorance and hatefulness by, for example, a sweet-voiced young woman with the air of having graduated from an expensive convent school about five minutes ago . . .

The famous surrealism or other-worldliness of Mexico is a tributary of Mexican Time. Here entirely serious and respectable people tell you about their encounters with ghosts, and I have learned to believe them, since I have had such encounters here myself, moments which have raised goosebumps in my flesh and a chill in my spine, and which I won't be so cursi as to try and elaborate on, much less attempt to justify. The surrealism I will describe this way: I used to, as a discipline, take long walks in this city, and I wouldn't turn back until I had seen something that astonished me. A found image of a character particular to Mexico City. I'm sure anyone who has lived here knows what I mean: the Manuel Alvarez Bravo images and moments that continue to proliferate all around us here. A beauty parlor on Calle Durango at four in the morning, the lights on through the curtains and bolero music coming from inside, and finding a wedge in the curtain to peek through, you see three middle-aged female beauticians, tequila bottles on the floor, getting plastered together. Those multi-liter bottles that purified drinking water gets delivered in, empty and lined up on a sidewalk next to a delivery truck, and one of the workers picking those bottles up and hurling them up into the air one at a time to the worker crouched atop the back of the truck: the way each bottle, tossed high into the air, fills for a moment with the spectacular bleeding colors of the smog-abetted sunset sky before dropping perfectly into the other's hands. This one, just the other day: a black

Francisco Goldman

Volkswagen bug from a driver's education school circling La Glorieta Citlatlepetl, going around and around, the grim-faced instructor seated on the right, and behind the wheel, the student just learning to drive: a man of about eighty, his silver hair elegantly slicked back, wearing a necktie, starched white shirt and dark suit for the occasion.

Stuart

From *The New Yorker*

> *"He lies like an eyewitness."*
> — Russian saying.

This is the truth, whichever way you look at it. There are these two Greek guys. One is as huge as hell, with a melon for a face: round, yellowish, moist, pitted with black-headed acne—and yet genial, all the same. It isn't exactly the kind of face the Italians call simpatico, but it's without malice, the way a melon is without malice. It is generous just because it is neutral, and neutral is a sight to behold in certain quarters of the city where men wear their features aggressively, like national flags. Comparatively speaking, this guy looks fine—despite a thick neck with a circumference beyond your handspan, beaded with sweat like the legendary boxers'. It is a triumph on his part not to look cruel. But then maybe he's just not rich enough to do cruel. Maybe cruel takes more money. As it is, he wears an XXL blue shirt of that cheap material that isn't really silk but reflects light and looks fancy—though what the label doesn't tell you is that it tends to be less subtle about body excretions. You'd think it must be worth a little more of anybody's money to avoid the battalion of sweat advancing from the armpits, the front-line grime on collars, on cuffs. But no. He chooses this cheap pseudo silk. He doesn't do himself any favors, either, by tucking it all into some tight, heavy-looking jeans. It is clear that this guy has a hard time with clothes in general; buying them, getting into them, getting out of them. Nothing quite fits. Even his apron looks stretched to its limits, the strings burrowed deep in his flanks, subsumed by the overhang. The apron itself decorates his belly with a colored sketch of five famous Greek things: the Acropolis, a kabob, Socrates, Zeus, and, finally, defiantly, the Elgin marbles. And he's got gold on his fingers: a large chunk of a ring stamped with a centaur, and an Irish claddagh ring—two spindly feminine hands clasped around his own hairy middle digit. For somebody who is preparing food for the public, his nails leave a lot to be desired.

The other guy, his partner, is about a foot shorter but just as wide, and he's mean-looking, which can often be a mere accident of physiognomy but other times proves to be right on the money. He is dressed roughly the same, except his apron claims that "Greek Men Do It Better," and he is sufficiently bull-browed and rivet-jawed to pull that sort of thing off. The two of them work a hot-dog stall with no name that you'd notice. The griddle is split among regular hot dogs, large hot dogs, and hamburgers. The onions are fried in a two-inch groove that runs horizontal along the front. The big melon-faced guy flips the burgers or turns the hot dogs, fries and refries the onions. The mono-browed mean-looking short guy scrapes the hot fat from one end of the griddle to the other with an egg slice, puts the meat in its respective bun, and squeezes the sauce bottles. Whoever has a hand free deals with the money. Wipes one hand on the corner of his apron, deals with the money. Exchanges coins, folds notes, opens and closes the cashbox—all with one hand. You can't get rich with this kind of enterprise, but Friday nights and school holidays keep your head above water. Everything runs pretty smoothly. Organized. Efficient. That's the only way to make it in this country. And you don't need to tell these guys that. There is a short red plastic tub on each side of their stand. The one on the right—their right—is for rubbish; the one on the left for napkins.

At about two o'clock, three white boys come into view. Fourteen, maybe fifteen years old. The small one might be thirteen. It's hard to tell from this angle; none of them can call puberty an old friend, a force of good firmly on their side. They have baby-blond womanish sideburns on their faces; not even sideburns, wisps of hair made darker and more substantial by hair products and—who knows?—maybe toothpaste. They have man-sized hands sprouting from elongated, spindly limbs like the extremities of flamingos, and their feet are so huge they might be prehensile; these kids might have just swung into town. There's nothing in the backside of their immense, baggy jeans, no backside to speak of, just air, and possibly this is an evolutionary development, for they are rarely to be found sitting down; they are always in a pack and on the move—they need backsides the way the rest of us need tails. Likelihood is they didn't pass an exam among them this summer, but their bodies are clever and have been adapting from the inside, silently, almost imperceptibly at first, confounding parents and politicians. These are not the bodies of boys a hundred years ago, or even thirty years ago. These boys are new. They wear a yellow shirt, a pink shirt, and a blue shirt, respectively, and this is how they will have to be identified, because their shoes (white trainers) and haircuts (short, greased, quiffed) are uniform; each has a can of beer lolling in his Mickey Mouse mitt, and two of them are the same coloring and height. They don't address each other by name. They know each other too well.

"Hot dog, mate," says the yellow shirt, and the smaller Greek takes one out and throws it on the griddle without a word. At some stands you're asked for the money first. Other stands want the money at the same time the hot dog's picked up. If they believe in building trust they might ask for the money after the hot dog is across the counter. These two particular Greeks seem to play it by ear, depending on how they feel about the customer. There is good feeling, for now. They don't mention money yet.

The pink shirt says, "Three hot dogs, mate. Three, yeah? Quick as you can, mate."

He looks over his shoulder. "Before they fucking catch up with us, eh?" he says to his friends, laughing. They all laugh.

"Nice day for it, eh?" says the yellow shirt, motioning to the sun, Mediterranean in September. The big Greek smiles and nods. "Indian summer," he replies. He tears open the plastic bag where the meat is kept. Two hot dogs sidle up to the first.

Then a group of little girls, none older than nine, comes round the corner, indeterminable in number because they move so quickly toward these older boys, pull at their legs, crowd round them, and begin twittering all at once. Most of them are black, with long eyelashes and com-

Zadie Smith

plicated hair. They all want hot dogs. They all want the older boys to buy them hot dogs.

"School holiday, eh?" says the bigger Greek, sympathizing. "You got to keep an eye on them?"

The pink shirt, eyelids not under his control, drunk in the afternoon, nods in the direction of the housing estate on the horizon, a long wide tetrahedron that declines in stages, balcony under balcony, in a slope like a giant staircase. This is where they come from.

"Mate, they just *follow* us," he says, grinning. "For fuck *sake*. I fuckin' *told* ya, didn't I?" he says irritably to a small white girl, a girl with similar watery green eyes, possibly his sister. "Take this lot with you and go and find something to do. No, I ain't buyin' you nuffink. Get out of it."

But they won't go and he gets into a debate with them, holding his head with one hand, his beer with the other. He's trying to explain. Meanwhile, his friends look sheepish, swig from their cans, kicking their feet against the curb.

"Fuckin' hell, man," says the yellow shirt. "I can't deal wiv this. We shouldn'ta come for hot dogs. Should've gone straight to the fucking pub, innit? They can't follow us in *there*. I can't take this, man. Just gonna ... yeah?" He gestures round the next corner, away from the girls. "Yeah?"

The pink shirt is down at the girls' level, crouching, not really listening. And then there is the street noise that swallows certain words, stealing away dialogue, filing it between car exhausts and police sirens. So his friends slink off without him. Maybe for a smoke. Maybe for more beer. They move into the city, merge with it, casually, the way young men can—there is no suggestion that they won't come back or that they will or how long they might be. No one notices them leaving until they are gone. The big melon-faced guy is scraping some onions up from the groove and turning the three hot dogs. His partner, head down, splits open three rolls and now proceeds to brown them. The pink shirt is busy forming a compromise out of some bubble gum he finds in his pocket. He bribes the girls with the pack and watches them scoot off.

"And don't come back," he shouts after them, but with a smile in his voice. The girls are so fast and loose-limbed they hit their behinds with the soles of their own shoes.

So it's only now that the pink shirt notices the absence of his friends as he straightens up, puts his tongue on the roof of his mouth, and extends his bottom lip, intending to form a name beginning with "T" (Tommy? Tony? Tim?); stops, sighs, says "Fuck it" under his breath. The beer has made his eyes slower than his brain, and they play catch-up in their sockets as he moves his head first right then left. He looks out helplessly now, down, along, toward the corner his friends might have turned. His jaw is slack; he repeats his request for hot dogs, speaking in the direction of no one and giving in to a slur. Then his grip slips; the beer can falls to the floor.

"You pick that up, please."

There is a voice speaking to him with slight aggression, and the boy brings his head round with some effort to attend to it.

"You pick it up, please."

The kid doesn't want any trouble. He picks it up willingly, spilling a little, but making no complaint.

"Sorry, man," he says, getting a firmer hold on it. "There you go, mate," he says and launches the can toward the red tub on his right.

The big Greek sighs in a deep, deliberate way, fishing the beer can out of his tub of napkins, and the kid takes in a sharp breath, wondering if this is the end of the good feeling. He can see that even the big Greek's casual grip bruises the can, giving it an adolescent overbite, stretching the lip over the rest of it. The big Greek looks at the kid as he does this. Then, to make his point, he waits a beat and throws the can along the street, aiming for a mouthy black bin, an obedient bulldog called to heel next to a traffic light. "Napkins," he says, pointing to the napkins. "Bin," he says, pointing to the bin. But, for some reason best explained by aerodynamics, it doesn't work out like that. The can's busted lip hits the rim of the bin, and the can spins off, retraces its flight. Four feet from the stall, it collides with a passerby—another young man, with a swaggering, wide-legged walk and a suit that he *needs* to make him better than this kid in the pink shirt—and the can weeps piss-colored beer all over his trousers, soaking the right pocket.

Immediately, the big Greek tries to offer hot dogs. It's the only currency he has. He gestures desperately to the three shimmying in their skins, popping in their own fat, those earmarked for the pink shirt, the blue shirt, and the yellow shirt, while his partner approaches the young man, apologetic, carrying napkins, as eager to dab the man as the man is to avoid him. He keeps repeating two sentences: *It's these kids, they don't respect nothing* and *Have what you like, free, on us.*

While, soaked and furious, the other guy plays his own scratched record: *If my phone's fucked, someone's fucking paying for it* and *I don't want your fucking hot dogs.*

Until it emerges that his phone is fine; he stalks off with it, phoning his secretary, saying, "Some cunt spilt beer all over my fucking...," turning the corner now, but still loud enough for the big Greek to hear how he is being described to somebody he will never meet. Maybe it is a woman. A white woman. Maybe she is beautiful, with long blond hair and teeth like in the ads. The big Greek, he's not cruel; he's not cruel like some guys in the city; but somebody's to blame for this latest humiliation, small but painful. Some blond woman he has never met will now never make love to him because he is just *some cunt*, selling hot dogs, spilling beer. She won't know that Greek Men Do It Better. She won't discover the truth: that while her ancestors were swinging through the trees his were writing great books and sculpting white bodies; bigger than men and smaller than the gods; halfway between here and heaven. The big Greek feels his face get hot. He feels sure he should have hurt that man for saying those things, but the opportunity has passed. In this city, you might miss your nemesis in a crowded shop in the morning and fight your friend in a park in the afternoon, never knowing your mistake. So he glares at the pink shirt. And the pink shirt prods his own chest, either side of the sternum, and then lowers his arms, his hands cupped as if holding two sandbags, a human scale, a defeated crucifix. The universal gesture for "Me?"

"Yes, you. What you think? I stand here all fucking day for my health? Who's going to take these? Where are the other two? Why you order if you not going to eat? You pay for three. Yes, you pay for three."

The kid remonstrates. And now the small mean-looking Greek steps into the arena.

"Yes, my friend, it's your fucking problem. It's not *our* fucking problem. Must be your fucking problem. Four-fifty now, please."

Once again, the pink shirt reaches for a word, the same old word. It is strange that even as the bodies evolve the language gets smaller and smaller—it is peculiar how few words you need to travel across town, get in a fight, ride the tube, buy a hot dog, fall in love. Here comes the same old word. Slowly, head back, teeth firmly planted in bottom lip, all facial muscles pulled tight: catapult face.

But something has snapped in the big genial Greek—this is the last day he can be spoken to like that, the last minute he can be genial in this city. It has finally broken him. From now on, when people ask him where he's from, he will have to think for a moment. Soon the answer *Greece* will feel as strange in his mouth as chalk. From now on, he's from *Here*, subject to all the daily cruelties of this place. And he's got the pink shirt by the collar now, before the kid has even opened his mouth. Next thing anybody knows, the kid's been hit, badly, across the nose, and it's bleeding and bent like in the movies. Peacekeepers and antagonizers appear in equal measure from nowhere, from invisible side streets, trying to put their hands on or between the action, and the big Greek's partner says, "Marios, Marios, *enough* now," trying to halt the taking off of the apron, because evidently Marios takes off his apron only when something serious occurs in his life. It is a signal of his intention to become more serious still. "Let the boy fight for himself," says Marios.

The pink shirt is on the ground, lamenting. He says, "He hit me! Fucker hit me for fucking *nothing!*" Doesn't look as if he'd ever been hit before. He can't get up because of the shock. He's crying and bleeding and snotting, and is choking on all three of these involuntary emissions. "These kids," says a spectator, a man leaning out of the mobile-phone shop next door. "All mouth and no trousers."

But here they come, the trousers, running balloon-legged as air rushes up the absence where a backside is meant to be; yellow shirt and blue shirt, at the scene, trying to process what eight or so eyewitnesses are shouting in unison, trying to listen to the testimony of their friend.

"He hit me!" explains the pink shirt again, incredulous. "I wasn't doing nuffink, he just hit me for no fucking reason!"

And it is this, in the end, that he can't understand; that someone should hit him for *no reason*, that things happen in the city for no reason, and blood can spring from nowhere. He's thinking, It's not *fair*. He's thinking about those guys in the papers—white shirt, green shirt, red shirt, pink shirt, orange shirt—who killed a black guy and got nothing, and here he is *minding his own business* with a nose pushed three centimetres to the left for his trouble.

"Fight!" shouts someone, describing what has just happened, inducing what is to come. On cue, the yellow shirt takes a wild swing at Marios, but Marios is without apron and Marios is too fast and fearless. His punch is a soaring sweeper with the ring hand and the centaur rides down the boy's cheek, slicing it open. The blood is a carmine red. Marios's ancestors were making wine that color, pouring it into goblets, comparing it to the sea, while everyone on this pavement was swinging from the trees.

"Come on then!" shouts Marios, beckoning the crowd with his fingertips, defying those who feel that hitting one child might be described as unfortunate but hitting two looks like malice. "Who wants some?"

No one—except maybe the blue shirt, who has resolved to be cunning, sneaking up behind the small mean Greek, and crushing his beer can on the back of his head. The small Greek flinches the way you flinch when someone plucks a hair from your head. And for a moment nothing happens. Then he turns. No one can be in any doubt now that this particular mean-looking short guy is a book that the wise man judges by its cover. He draws back his football of a fist. Everybody starts to run.

The blue shirt is first, obviously, followed closely by the small mean Greek, followed by the assembled chorus, which contains Marios, maybe also the yellow shirt—things are moving too fast to be sure. This is a tableau doing the hundred metres. The blue shirt runs as if Tyson were on his tail. High-foots it. Works his arms and pulls his knees up and keeps his head low like Linford Christie—just looking for the free pavement. It comes down to a hunt now, and though the small Greek has his two fists, his simple and effective city weaponry, the boy is darting like an okapi; jumps bins and weaves between push-chairs and shoppers and old people, down the high street, searching for any way out.

"I'll kill you!" says the small mean Greek. No one is in any doubt of that. No one stops running.

It's all a matter of being the first to see what's coming next. That's how you win in this country, any country. It's the blue shirt, the chasee, who is the first to understand that the hundred metres is going to turn into the four hundred metres, and he paces himself accordingly, while the small mean Greek, the chaser, struggles. And it is the blue shirt who first spots the final metamorphosis, from the four hundred metres to the hurdles, as they pass the crossroads and the second set of traffic lights and head directly for the three-foot iron railings that line the pavement outside McDonald's. It's just *elegant* the way he leaps them, barely breaking his stride, his legs in an "S" shape as he glides over, landing as firm as a Russian gymnast and turning the corner without slowing down. Leaps like that are what being fourteen is for. The small mean Greek is so transfixed by it that he, like everyone else in the street, ignores the street for a second, focussing only on this flying boy, who has been made supernatural for a moment by the extra six inches in the air that his fear and his youth have bestowed upon him.

The small mean Greek ignores the street like everyone else, thinking he will be safe like everyone else. But it is only he who is heading directly, unknowingly, for the tremendously fat man in the brown McDonald's uniform who is leaving work, pushing open the large glass doors, minding his own business with a Big Mac and large fries. An immense man. Three hundred pounds of a man. He barely walks, this man, but waddles; he needs to turn his feet out as much as possible just to stay upright. His long hair is in a ponytail, wet with sweat from root to tip. He's out of breath from the effort of crossing the road, and you get the feeling he's *always* out of breath. It's hard work being that weight in this city and keeping any dignity. You get stared at with pity and relief, because whatever the commuters have done today, no matter how shameful the act, it is put into perspective by the sight of you and others like you, fat and poor. Fat poor people are truly public television. And if this guy notices anything wrong as he bites into his burger it's just that he can't feel any eyes on him this afternoon. Something else must be happening on a different channel.

"Move!" shouts someone. But it's hard to save a man if you don't know his name. They're not close enough to see "Stuart***" on his nametag. Only three stars. Five stars are the most you can receive as a McDonald's employee. But Stuart*** is only an average McDonald's employee. Lord knows what he does wrong. Maybe his weight makes him unpleasant to the customers. Maybe he's slow with the coffee. Through the glass front of the restaurant, ten feet away, you can see that other servers are Somalian, or Indian, or Caribbean, and are in the five-star bracket. Maybe

Zadie Smith

they give five stars only to their own. No doubt Stuart*** has suspected this.

Jesus!

That is the sound from the crowd as the two men collide and Stuart*** goes up in the air, his belly moving like a giant beanbag, his whole form rising a foot, two feet from the ground, at least. *Christ* is the word as he lands, badly, horribly, as only a fat man can land. For even once he's hit the ground it is not over, as the force of the impact travels in waves through the loose flesh. And then a collective gasp occurs, the kind people believe to be a convention of the movies until it happens to them. Many of the women scream. The more responsible people, the people we would like to have running our hospitals and checking our gas heaters, look for the nearest phone and tentatively suggest first aid or that no one panic. The yellow shirt vomits where he stands. The small mean Greek kneels on the ground where he fell, looks to the heavens, and shouts something in his mother tongue.

"Oh God!" cries a woman, as if Stuart*** were her own child. "Oh God, oh God, oh God! I can't stand it!"

She means she can't stand the thought that blood can spring from nowhere, even when it isn't her own. But you've got to be tougher than this woman if you want to survive in this country, any country. "Somebody call an ambulance!" she says, though she knows in all probability that somebody already has.

This is the truth, whichever way you look at it: Stuart*** needs an ambulance right now. Stuart***'s stubby sausage of a right leg is bent backward at the knee. His foot is back-to-front. He is faced with his own heel like a puppet doing the cancan. His whole body reverberates with the pain. You can tell, because he's shaking like a Mexican jumping bean. He can't cry, because he hasn't even got that far. He hasn't got as far as *consequences*. He's still sitting in the *event*. Yet already he has passed into anecdote, and those who didn't see it are being told about it by those who did, putting more pounds on him than his frame can hold, placing him higher in the air than a man can go. People will go home this evening and phone their friends. People will elaborate over dinner. And it might serve to stave off an awkward silence between colleagues tomorrow morning as the train rumbles on from the end of the line to the middle of town. For a brief time, sitting in the street stopping the traffic, Stuart*** becomes the center of the city, the median coordinate, a dubious honor he never hoped for nor expected to receive. He is in enough pain for the entire city. Everybody watches him begin to hyperventilate and dig his fingers into his stomach, searching for where it hurts, for where the hurt begins. Someone should tell him he'll split his lip if he keeps biting down on it like that. Stuart***'s eyes are closed. He will be the last person to see what has happened to him.

Louise Erdrich

Revival Road

From *The New Yorker*

From the air, our road must look like a length of rope flung down haphaz-ardly, a thing of inscrutable loops and half-finished question marks. But there is a design to Revival Road. The beginning of the road is paved, though with a material inferior to that of the main highway, which snakes south from our college town into the villages and factory cities of New Hampshire. When the town has the money, the road is also coated with light gravel. Over the course of a summer, those bits of stone are pressed into the softened tar, making a smooth surface on which the cars pick up speed. By midwinter, though, the frost has crept beneath the road and flexed, creating heaves that force the cars to slow again. I'm glad when that happens, for children walk down this road to the bus stop be-low. They walk past our house with their dogs, wearing puffy jackets of saturated brilliance—hot pink, hot yellow, hot blue. They change shape and grow before my eyes, becoming the young drivers of fast cars that barely miss the smaller children, who, in their turn, grow up and drive away from here.

One day in the dead of winter, one of these young drivers appeared at our door, knocking so frantically that my mother called to me in alarm. I came rushing from the basement laundry room to see him standing be-hind the glass of the back storm door, jacketless and shivering. I saw that he was missing a finger from the hand he raised, and recognized him as the Eyke boy, now grown, years past fooling with his father's chainsaw. But not his father's new credit-bought car. Davan Eyke had sneaked his father's automobile out for an illicit spin and lost control as he came down the hill beside our house. The car had slid toward a steep gully lined with birch and, by lucky chance, had come to rest pinned precisely between two trunks. The trees now held the expensive and unpaid-for white car in a perfect vise. Not one dent. Not one silvery scratch. Not yet. It was Davan's hope that if I hooked a chain to my Subaru and backed up the hill I would be able to pull his car gently free.

My chain snapped. So did many others over the course of the afternoon. At the bottom of the road, a collection of cars, trucks, equipment, and people gathered. As the car was unwedged, as it was rocked, yanked, pushed, and released, as other ideas were tried and discarded, and as the newness of the machine wore off, Davan saw that his plan had failed and he began to despair. With empty eyes, he watched a dump truck winch his father's vehicle half free, then slam it flat on its side and drag it shrieking up a lick of gravel that the town's road agent had laid down for traction.

Over the years our town, famous for the softness and drama of its natural light, has drawn artists from the large cities of the Eastern Seaboard. Most of them have had some success in the marketplace, and since New Hampshire does not tax income—preferring a thousand other less effective ways to raise revenue—they find themselves wealthier here, albeit slightly bored. For company, they are forced to rely on locals such as myself—a former schoolteacher, fired for insubordination, a semi-educated art lover. Down at the end of our road, in a large brick Cape attached to a white clapboard carriage house (now a studio), there lives such an artist.

Kurt Heissman is a striking man, formerly much celebrated for his assemblages of stone, but now mainly ignored. He hasn't produced a major piece in years. His works often incorporate massive pieces of native slate or granite, and he occasionally hires young local men to help with their execution. His assistants live on the grounds—there is a small cottage sheltered by an old white pine—and are required to be available for work at any time of the day or night. There is no telling when the inspiration to fit one stone in a certain position upon another may finally strike.

Heissman favors the heavy plaid woollens sold by mail, and his movements are ponderous and considered. His gray hair is cut in a brushy crewcut, the same do that Uncle Sam once gave him. Though he complains about his loss of energy, he is in remarkable health at fifty. His hands are oddly, surprisingly, delicate and small. His feet are almost girlish in their neatly tied boots, a contrast to the rest of him, so boldly cut and rugged. I have heard that the size of a man's hands and feet is an accurate predictor of the size of his sex, but with Kurt Heissman this does not prove to be the case. If this statement is crude, that is of no concern to me—I am citing a fact. I love the way this man is made.

The stones that he gathers for possible use intrigue me. I think I know, sometimes, what it is about them that draws him. He says that the Japanese have a word for the essence apparent in a rock, and I suppose that I love him for his ability to see that essence. I wish sometimes that I were stone. Then he would see me as I am: peach-colored granite with flecks of angry mica. My balance is slightly off. I am leaning toward him, farther, farther. Should I try to right myself? This is not an aesthetic choice.

When Davan Eyke was forced to leave home after the accident, he did not go far, just up to Kurt Heissman's little guest cottage beneath the boughs of the beautiful, enfolding pine. The tree has an unusually powerful shape, and Heissman and I have speculated often on its age. We are both quite certain that it was small, a mere sapling, too tender to bother with, when the agents of the English king first marked the tallest and straightest trees in the forests of New England as destined for the shipyards of the Royal Navy, where they would become masts from which to hang great sails. Any large pine growing now was a seedling when the pine canopy, so huge and dense that no light shone onto the centuries of bronze needles below, was axed down. This tree splits, halfway up its trunk, into three parts that form an enormous crown. In that crotch there is a raven's nest, which is unusual, since ravens are shy of Northeasterners, having a long collective memory for the guns, nets, and poisons with which they were once almost eradicated.

The ravens watched when Davan Eyke moved in, but they watch everything. They are humorous, highly intelligent birds, and knew immediately that Davan Eyke would be trouble. Therefore they disturbed his sleep by dropping twigs and pinecones on the painted tin roof of his cottage; they shat on the lintel, stole small things he left in the yard—pencils, coins, his watch—and hid them. They also laughed. The laughter of a raven is a sound unendurably human. You may know it, if you have heard it in your own throat, as the noise of that peculiarly German word *Schadenfreude*. Perhaps the raven's laughter, its low rasp, reminds us of the depth of our own human darkness. Of course, there is nothing human about it and its source is unknowable, as are the hearts of all things wild. Davan Eyke was bothered, though, enough so that he complained to Heissman about the birds.

"Get used to them" was all the artist said to Davan Eyke.

Heissman tells me this one day as I bring him the mail, a thing I do often when he feels close to tossing himself into the throes of some ambitious piece. At those times, he cannot or will not break the thread of his concentration by making a trip to the post office. There is too much at stake. This could be the day that his talent will resurrect itself painfully from the grief into which it has been plunged.

"I have in mind a perception of balance, although the whole thing must be brutally off the mark and highly dysphoric." He speaks like this—pompous, amused at his own pronouncements, his eyes brightening beneath their heavy white brows.

"Awkward," I say, to deflate him. "Maybe even ugly."

In his self-satisfaction there is more than a hint of the repressed Kansas farm boy he was when he first left home for New York City. That boy is buried under many layers now—there is a veneer of faked European ennui, an aggressive macho crackle, an edge of judgmental Lutheranism, and a stratum of terrible sadness over the not so recent loss of his second wife, who was killed in a car accident out West.

"Do you know," Heissman said once, "that a stone can be wedged just so into the undercarriage of a car that, when you press the gas pedal, it sticks and shoots the car forward at an amazing speed?" That was the gist of the fluke occurrence that had killed his wife. A high-school prank in

Montana, near Flathead Lake. Stones on the highway. As she pressed on the brakes, Heissman says, her speed increased. Not a beautiful woman, in her pictures, but forceful, intelligent, athletic. She is resembled by their daughter, Freda, a girl who seems to have committed herself to dressing in nothing but black and purple since she entered Sarah Lawrence. When Heissman speaks of Freda's coming home for a weekend, his voice is tender, almost dreamy. At those times, it has a kind of yearning that I would do anything to hear directed toward me. I'm jealous. That is just the way it is. I tell myself that he sees Freda not as his actual self-absorbed and petulant daughter but as the incarnation of his lost wife. But I don't like Freda and she doesn't like me.

"He's not working out," Heissman says now, of Davan Eyke. "I shouldn't hire locals."

I shrug off his use of the word "local." After all, I am one, although I qualify in Heissman's mind as both local and of the larger world, since I spent several years in London, living in fearful solitude on the edge of Soho and failing my degree.

"You wouldn't have to hire anybody if you used smaller rocks," I answer, my voice falsely dismissive.

Our friendship is based, partly, on the pretense that I do not take his work, or his failure to work, seriously, and do not mind whether we are sexual or not, when in fact we both know that I value his work and am quietly, desperately, with no hope of satisfaction, in love with him. He believes that I am invulnerable. I protect myself with every trick I know.

"This guy's a brainless punk," Heissman continues.

"I thought you knew that when you hired him."

"I suppose I could have told by looking at him, but I didn't really look."

"The only job he's ever had was cutting grass, and half the time he broke the lawnmower. He broke so many on this road that people stopped hiring him. Still," I tell Heissman, "he's not a bad person, not even close to bad. He's just ..." I try to get at the thing about Eyke. "He doesn't care about anything." My defense is lame, and my lover does not buy it.

"I was desperate. I was working on 'Construction No. 20.' "

"No. 20" is the working title of a piece commissioned many, many years ago by a large Minneapolis cereal company for its corporate grounds. It is still not finished.

Davan Eyke appears, and I stay and watch the two men wrestle steel and stone. Eyke looks slight next to his boss. Together, though, they haul stones from the woods, drag and lever blocks of pale marble delivered from the Rutland quarries. If Davan were artistic, this would be an ideal job, a chance to live close to and learn from a master. As it is, Davan's enthusiasm quickly gives way to the resentment he transfers from his father to his boss.

My mother sighs and makes a face when I tell her that Freda Heissman is visiting her father, and that he has invited us to dinner. Heissman often invites us to dinners that do not happen once Freda becomes involved. She rails against me; I suspect that she has prevailed upon her father more than once to break off our friendship. There is a low energy to Freda, a fantastic kind of drama, a way of doing ordinary things with immense conviction. When I first met her, it was hard to believe that the dots she splashed on paper, the C-plus science projects she displayed with such bravura were only adequate. Looking at her through the lens of her dead mother's image, however, Heissman is convinced that she is extraordinary.

I shouldn't be so hard on Freda, I suppose. But is it proper for the young to be so disappointing? And Heissman—why can't he see? I have dearly wished that she'd find a boyfriend for herself, and yet our sense of class distinction in this country is so ingrained that neither of us had considered Davan Eyke, either to dismiss or encourage such a match. There he was, sullenly enduring his surroundings, winging pebbles at the tormenting birds, but since he was not of the intelligentsia (such as we are) who live on Revival Road, he didn't occur to us.

This is the sort of family he is from: The Eykes. His father is a tinkering, sporadically employed mechanic. His mother drives the local gas truck. In their packed-earth yard, a dog was tied for many years, a lovely thing, part German shepherd and part husky, one eye brown and one blue. The dog was never taken off a short chain that bound it to the trunk of a tree. It lived in that tiny radius through all weathers, lived patiently, enduring each dull moment of its life, showing no hint of going mean.

I suppose I am no better than the Eykes. I called the Humane Society once, but when no one came and the dog still wound the chain one way and then the other, around and around the tree, I did nothing more. Rather than confronting the Eykes—which seemed unthinkable to me, since Mr. Eyke not only hauled away our trash but mowed our field and kept the trees in good condition by plucking away the tall grasses at their trunks—I was silent. From time to time, I brought the dog a bone when I passed, and felt a certain degree of contempt for the Eykes, as one does for people who mistreat an animal.

That is one failure I regret having to do with the Eykes. The other is my shortsightedness regarding Davan and Freda.

A turbulent flow of hormones runs up and down this road. On my walks, I've seen adolescence bolt each neighbor child upward like a sun-drunk plant. Most of the houses on the road are surrounded by dark trees and a tangle of undergrowth. No two are within shouting distance. Yet you *know*, merely by waving to the parents whose haunted eyes bore through the windshields of their cars. You hear, as new trail bikes and motorbikes rip the quiet, as boom boxes blare from their perches on newly muscled shoulders. The family cars, once so predictable in their routes, buck and raise dust as they race up and down the hill. This is a painful time, and you avert your eyes from the houses that contain it. The very foundations of those homes seem less secure. Love falters and blows. Steam rises from the ditches, and sensible neighbors ask no questions.

Davan hit like that, a compact freckled boy who suddenly grew long-jawed and reckless. Mother says that she knew it was the end when he started breaking lawnmowers, slamming them onto the grass and stones so savagely that the blades bent. She quietly had our mower fixed and did not hire him again. His brown hair grew until it reached his shoulders, and a new beard came in across his chin like streaks of dirt. Frighteningly, Davan walked the road from time to time, dressed in camouflage, hugging his father's crossbow and arrows, with which he transfixed woodchucks. That phase passed, and then he lapsed into a stupor of anger that lasted for years and culminated in the damage he did to his father's new car by driving it into the trees. It was the most expensive thing his family had ever bought, and since he left home soon after that, it was clear he was not forgiven.

Freda Heissman, on the other hand, had resolved her adolescence beautifully. After a few stormy junior-high-school years following her mother's death, she settled into a pattern of achieving small things with great flair, for, as I mentioned, she had no talents and was at most a mediocre student. She gave the impression that she was going places, though, and so she did go places. Still, her acceptance into a prestigious college was a mystery to all who knew her. Her teachers, including me, were stymied. Perhaps it was the interview, one woman told my mother.

Later, in the seething, watery spring darkness, Heissman enters our house via the back-porch screen door, to which he has the key. It is the only door of the house that unlocks with that key, and I keep things that way for the following reason: should I tire, should I have the enlightenment or the self-discipline or the good sense to stop Heissman from coming to me in the night, it will be a simple matter. One locksmith's fee. One tossed key. No explanation owed. Though my mother must sense, must conjecture, must know without ever saying so that Heissman's night visits occur, we do not speak of it and never have. Her room is at the other end of the house. We live privately, in many respects, and although this is how we prefer to live, there are times when I nearly spill over with the need to confide my feelings.

For when he steps into my room it is as though I am waking on some strange and unlikely margin. As though the ocean has been set suddenly before me. Landlocked, you forget. Then, suddenly, you are wading hip high into the surge of waves. There is so much meaning, so much hunger in our mouths and skin. This is happiness, I think every time. I've had lovers, several, and what I like best is the curious unfolding confessional quality of sex. I seek it, demand it of Heissman, and for a matter of hours he is bare to me, all candor and desire. He begs things of me. *Put your mouth here.* In nakedness we are the reverse of our day selves.

Ravens are the birds I'll miss most when I die. If only the darkness into which we must look were composed of the black light of their limber in-

Louise Erdrich

telligence. If only we did not have to die at all and instead became ravens. I've watched these birds so hard that I feel their black feathers split out of my skin. To fly from one tree to another, the raven hangs itself, hawklike, on the air. I hang myself that same way in sleep, between one day and the next. When we're young, we think we are the only species worth knowing. But the more I come to know people, the better I like ravens. In this house, open to a wide back field and pond, I am living within their territory. A few years ago, there were eight or more of them in Heissman's white pine. Now just four live there, and six live somewhere in the heavy fringe of woods beyond my field. Two made their nest in the pine. Three hatchlings were reared. The other raven was killed by Davan Eyke.

You may wonder how on earth an undisciplined, highly unpleasant, not particularly coordinated youth could catch and kill a raven. They are infernally cautious birds. For instance, having long experience with poisoned carcasses, they will not take the first taste of dead food but let the opportunistic blue jays eat their fill. Only when they see that the bold, greedy jays have survived do the ravens drive them off and settle in to feed. Davan had to use his father's crossbow to kill a raven. One day when Heissman was gone, he sat on the front stoop of his little cottage and waited for the birds to gather in their usual circle of derision. As they laughed at him among themselves, stepping through the branches, he slowly raised the crossbow. They would have vanished at the sight of a gun. But they were unfamiliar with other instruments. They did not know the purpose or the range of the bow. One strayed down too far, and Davan's arrow pierced it completely. Heissman drove into the yard and saw Davan standing over the bird. Amazingly, it wasn't dead. With some fascination, Davan was watching it struggle on the shaft of the arrow, the point of which was driven into the earth. Heissman walked over, snapped the arrow off, and drew it tenderly, terribly, from the bird's body. For a moment the raven sprawled, limp, on the ground, and then it gathered itself, walked away, and entered the woods to die. Overhead and out of range, the other birds wheeled. For once, they were silent.

"Let me see the bow," Heissman said conversationally. Davan handed it to him, prepared to point out its marvellous and lethal features. "And the arrows." Davan handed those over, too. "I'll be right back," Heissman said.

Davan waited. Heissman walked across the yard to his woodpile, turned, and fitted an arrow into the groove. Then he raised the bow. Davan stepped aside, looked around for the target, looked uneasily back at Heissman, then touched his own breast as the sculptor lifted the shoulder piece. *Shot.* Davan leapt to the other side of the white pine and vaulted off into the brush. The arrow stuck in the tree, just behind his shoulder. Then Heissman laid the bow on the block he used to split his firewood. He axed the weapon neatly in half. He laid the arrows down next, like a bunch of scallions, and chopped them into short lengths. He walked into his house and phoned me. "If you see that boy running past your house," he said, "here's why."

"You shot at him?"

"Not to hit him."

"But still, my God."

Heissman, embarrassed, did not speak of this again.

Davan had saved enough money, from Heissman's pay (or so we thought), to buy himself an old Toyota, dusty red with a splash of dark rust on the door where a dent had raised metal through the paint. The car now spewed grit and smoke on the road as he drove it back and forth to town. He had returned to his room in his parents' house and he resumed his chore of feeding the dog every day, though he never untied it from the tree.

The dog's maple grew great patches of liver-colored moss and dropped dead limbs. Shit-poisoned, soaked with urine at the base, and nearly girdled by the continual sawing and wearing of the chain, the tree had, for years, yellowed and then blazed orange, unhealthily, the first of all the trees on the road. Then, one day that spring, it fell over, and the dog walked off calmly, like the raven, into the woods, dragging a three-foot length of chain. Only the dog didn't die. Perhaps it had been completely mad all along, or perhaps it was that moment after the tree went down when, unwrapping itself nervously, the dog took one step beyond the radius of packed dirt within which it had lived since it was a fat puppy. Perhaps that step, the paw meeting grass, rang along the spine of the dog, fed such new light into its brain that it could not contain the barrage of information. At any rate, the outcome of that moment wasn't to be seen for

Louise Erdrich

several weeks, by which time Davan had successfully raised dust near Freda on illicit visits, and had secretly taken her out with him to local parties, where at first she enjoyed her status as a college-goer and the small sensation caused by her New York clothing styles. Then, at some point, something awakened in her, some sense of pity or conscience. Before that, I'd seen nothing remarkable about Heissman's daughter, other than her clothes. Her unkindness, her laziness, her feeling of enormous self-worth—all were typical of women her age. Then, suddenly, she had this urge to care for and rescue Davan Eyke, an abrupt unblocking of compassion which made her come clean with her father, a humanity that thoroughly terrified Heissman.

I step out of the car with the mail and see Heissman standing, blocklike, in front of Davan, who slouches before the older man with obdurate weariness. Locked in their man-space, they do not acknowledge me. Heissman is, of course, telling Davan Eyke that he doesn't want him to see Freda. He probably calls Davan some name, or makes some threat, for Davan steps back and stares at him alertly, hands up, as though ready to block a punch, which never comes. Heissman kicks him over, instead, with a rageful ease that astonishes Davan Eyke. From the ground, he shakes his head in puzzlement at Heissman's feet. When Heissman draws his leg back to kick again, I move forward. The kick stops midway. Davan rises. The two stare at each other with spinning hatred—I can almost see the black web between them.

"Pay me," Davan says, backing away.

"Say you won't see her first."

Davan starts to laugh, raucous, crackling, a raven's laugh. I can still hear it through the car window when he revs and peels out.

I don't understand why Heissman detests the boy so much; it is as though he has tapped some awful gusher in the artist and now, in a welter of frustrated energy, Heissman starts working. He finishes "No. 20." He produces, hardly sleeps. Hardly sees me.

It is difficult for a woman to admit that she gets along with her own mother. Somehow, it seems a form of betrayal. So few do. To join in the company of women, to be adults, we go through a period of proudly boasting of having survived our mothers' indifference, anger, overpowering love, the burden of their pain, their tendency to drink or teetotal, their warmth or coldness, praise or criticism, sexual confusion or embarrassing clarity. It isn't enough that our mothers sweated, labored, bore their daughters nobly or under total anesthesia or both. No. They must be responsible for our psychic weaknesses for the rest of their lives. It is all right to forgive our fathers. We all know that. But our mothers are held to a standard so exacting that it has no principles. They simply must be to blame.

I reject that, as my mother sits before me here. She has just had an operation to restore her vision. Her eyes are closed beneath small plastic cups and gauze bandages. When I change the gauze and put in the drops twice a day, it strikes me that there is something in the nakedness of her face and shut eyes that is like that of a newborn animal. Her skin has always been extremely clean and fine. Often, she has smelled to me of soap, but now she has added a light perfume, which enables her in her blindness to retrace her steps through the house with confidence, by smell.

That is how I know that she knows he has been here. Last night, he came down off the manic high in which he had hung between one uninspired month and the next. It is morning. Even to me, the house smells different after Heissman has made love to me in the night, more alive, alert with a fresh exquisite maleness. Still, for me to openly become Heissman's lover would upset the balance of our lives. My deadlocked secret love and unsecret contempt are the only hold I have over him, my only power. So things remain as they are. My mother and I maintain a calm life together. I do not dread, as others might, her increasing dependence. It is only that I have the strange, unadult wish that if she must pass into death, that rough mountain, she take me with her. Not leave me scratching at the shut seam of stone.

Spring on this road commences with a rush of dark rain, slick mud, and then dry warmth, which is bad for our wells and ponds but wonderful to see in the woods. New sounds, the rapturous trilling of peepers, that electric sexual whine, the caterwauling of the barred owls, startling us from sleep, raising bubbles of tension in my blood. I cannot imagine myself

Louise Erdrich

changing the lock. Without a word, without a sound, I circle Heissman, dragging my chain.

All of March, there is no sign of the dog that slipped free of the dead maple, and Mother and I can only assume that it has been taken in somewhere as a stray or, perhaps, shot from a farmer's back porch for running deer. That is how it probably survives—if it does—squeezing through a hole in the game-park fence, living on hand-raised pheasants and winter-killed carcasses.

The dog reappears in the full blush of April. During that week, leaves shoot from buds and the air films over with a bitter and intangible green that sweetens and darkens in so short a time. One balmy night, my neighbors up the road, the ones who clear-cut fifty acres of standing timber in four shocking days, have their cocker spaniel eaten. They leave the dog out all night on its wire run, and the next morning, from the back door, Ann Flaud in her nightgown pulls the dog's lead toward her. It rattles across the ground. At the end of it hangs an empty collar, half gnawed through.

There is little else to find. Just a patch of blood and the two long, mitteny brown ears. Coydogs are blamed—those mythical creatures invoked for every loss—then Satanists. I know it is the dog. I have seen her at the edge of our field, loping on long springy wolf legs. She does not look starved. She is alive—fat, glossy, huge.

She takes a veal calf for supper one night, pulled from its standup torture pen at the one working farm on the road that survived the eighties. She steals suet out of people's bird feeders, eats garbage, meadow voles, and frogs. A few cats disappear. She is now seen regularly, never caught. People build stout fences around their chicken pens. It is not until she meets the school bus, though, mouth open, the sad eye of liquid brown and the hungry eye of crystal blue trained on the doors as they swish open, that the state police become involved.

A dragnet of shotgun-armed volunteers and local police fans through the woods. Parked on this road, an officer with a vague memory of a car theft in Concord runs a check on Davan Eyke's red car as it flashes past. Eyke is on his way up to Heissman's, where Freda, less boldly attired than usual and biting black lacquer from her nails, waits to counsel him. They go for a walk in the woods, leaving the car in the driveway, in full view of Heissman's studio. They return, and then, despite Heissman's express, uncompromising, direct orders, Freda does exactly what young people sometimes do—the opposite. The human heart is every bit as tangled as our road. She gets into the car with Eyke.

On the police check, the car turns up stolen, and as it speeds back down from Heissman's an hour later the police officer puts on his siren and spins out in pursuit. There ensues a dangerous game of tag that the newspapers will call a high-speed chase. On our narrow roads, filled with hairpin turns, sudden drops, and abrupt hills, speed is a harrowing prospect. Davan Eyke tears down the highway, hangs a sharp left on Tapper Road, and jumps the car onto a narrow gravel path used mainly for walking horses. He winds up and down the hill like a slingshot, joins the wider road, then continues toward Windsor, over the country's longest covered bridge, into Vermont, where, at the first stoplight, he screeches between two cars in a sudden left-hand turn against the red. On blacktop now, the car is clocked at over a hundred miles per hour. There isn't much the police can do but follow as fast as they dare.

Another left, and it seems that Davan is intent on fleeing back toward Claremont, on the New Hampshire side. The police car radios ahead as he swings around a curve on two wheels and makes for the bridge that crosses the wide, calm Connecticut, which serves as a boundary between New Hampshire and Vermont. It is a cold, wet, late-spring afternoon, and, according to the sign that blurs before Davan's eyes, the bridge is liable to freeze before the road. It has. The car hits ice at perhaps a hundred and twenty and soars straight over the low guardrail. A woman in the oncoming lane says later that the red car was travelling at such a velocity that it seemed to gain purchase in the air and hang above the river. She also swears that she saw, before the car flew over, the white flower of a face pressing toward the window. No one sees a thing after that, although the fisherman pulling his boat onto shore below the bridge is suddenly aware of a great shadow behind him, as though a cloud has fallen out of the sky or a bird has touched his back lightly with its wing. He turns too slowly, even in his panic, to see anything but the river in its timeless run. The impact of the small car on the water is so tremendous that there is no ripple to mark its passage from a state of movement to complete arrest. It is as though the car and its passengers are simply atomized, reduced instantaneously to their elements.

Within fifteen minutes of the radio call, all the pickups and cars on our road gather their passengers and firearms and sweep away from the dog posse to the scene of greater drama at the bridge. Although the wreckage isn't found for days and requires four wet-suited divers to locate and gather, the police make a visit to Heissman's, on the strength of the woman witness's story. Believing that Freda has gone over the bridge as well, they take me along to break the news to my friend.

I wait on the edge of the field for Heissman, my hand on the stump of an old pine's first limb. I hear the ravens deep in the brush, the grating *haw-haw* of their announcement, and it occurs to me that he might just show up with Freda. But he doesn't, only shambles toward me alone at my call. I feel for the first time in our mutual life that I am invested with startling height, even power, perhaps more intelligence than I am used to admitting I possess. I feel a sickening omnipotence.

He starts at my naked expression, asks, "What?"

"Davan's car," I report, "went over the bridge."

I don't know what I expect, then, from Heissman. Anything but his offhand, strangely shuttered nonreaction. He apparently has no idea that Freda could be in the car. Unable to go on, I fall silent. For all his sullen gravity, Davan had experienced and expressed only a shy love for Heissman's daughter. It was an emotion he was capable of feeling, as was the fear that made him press the gas pedal. *The gas pedal*, I think. *The gas pedal and the wedged-in stone.*

I stare at Heissman. My heart creaks shut. I turn away from him and walk into the woods. At first, I think I'm going off to suffer like the raven, but as I walk on and on I know that I will be fine and I will be loyal, pathologically faithful. The realization grounds me. I feel more alive. The grass cracks beneath each step I take and the sweet dry dust of it stirs around my ankles. In a long, low swale of a field that runs into a dense pressure of trees, I stop and breathe carefully.

Whenever you leave cleared land, when you step from some place carved out, plowed, or traced by a human and pass into the woods, you must leave something of yourself behind. It is that sudden loss, I think, even more than the difficulty of walking through undergrowth, that keeps people firmly fixed to paths. In the woods, there is no right way to go, of course, no trail to follow but the law of growth. You must leave behind the notion that things are right. Just look around you. Here is the way things are. Twisted, fallen, split at the root. What grows best does so at the expense of what's beneath. A white birch feeds on the pulp of an old hemlock and supports the grapevine that will slowly throttle it. In the dead wood of another tree grow fungi black as devil's hooves. Overhead the canopy, tall pines that whistle and shudder and choke off light from their own lower branches.

The dog is not seen and never returns to Revival Road, never kills another spaniel or chicken, never appears again near the house where her nature devolved, never howls in the park, and never harms a child. Yet at night, in bed, my door unlocked, as I wait I imagine that she pauses at the edge of my field, suspicious of the open space, then lopes off with her length of chain striking sparks from the exposed ledge and boulders. I have the greatest wish to stare into her eyes, but if I should meet her face to face, breathless and heavy-muzzled, shining with blood, would the brown eye see me or the blue eye?

He has weakened, Heissman, he needs me these days. My mother says, out of nowhere, *He's not who you think he is.* I touch her shoulders, reassuringly. She shrugs me off because she senses with disappointment that I actually do know him, right down to the ground. Shame, pleasure, ugliness, loss: they are the heat in the night that tempers the links. And then there is forgiveness when a person is unforgivable, and a man weeping like a child, and the dark house soaking up the hollow cries.

J o h n   F r a z i e r

Interglacial

From *Callaloo*

We are still in an ice age.
Saturday morning, Museum of Natural History

with a man twice my lover, twice
my ex-lover. Ice ages are rhythmic,

marked by periods of warmth and cold,
partly ruled by geographies breaking or coming

together.

                              Who knows

our guide questions when the Earth will cool
again? In two hours

we will begin making love on the small sofa.
One of us will stop. One will continue. We will

both stop, pull away, start,
stop again, stuff our cocks into

our shorts, brew the mint tea bought at market,
let it steep.

James Ellis Thomas

The Saturday Morning Car Wash Club

From *The New Yorker*

To be sixteen on a July Saturday was heaven. Our neighborhood really showed out in the summer. Chumps who dragged ass to work all week leaped out of bed on Saturday mornings—it was the best way to cheat the heat. A lawnmower, a grill, a chair beneath a shade tree, anything that involved making something out of nothing powered their need to rise. Even the ne'er-do-wells started early on a Saturday. You'd see guys who hadn't caught a weather report in years strolling about like businessmen, on their way to trade chat with their down-the-block neighbors. My mother always said that Pig and Sammy Sam, our local hopheads, liked to get out early on a Saturday because then no one could tell them to go get a job. "It's Saturday!" Pig would say. "Unemployment office closed on Saturday!"

Most fellas between sixteen and married spent their weekend mornings at the Saturday Morning Car Wash Club. Actually, it wasn't really a club, just a run-down, semi-automated car wash two blocks up from Cedar Heights. The structure itself was ugly. Faded, cracked, and tornado-abused, it looked like a pistol-whipped tin man, surrounded by kudzu and non-biodegradables from the Burger King uphill. It was green. The hoses all had leaks in them. The vacuum cleaners were from the seventies, and the change machine was still chewing on the counterfeit five that Pig had fed it two years ago. Yet this did not stop the solitary ride from pulling up to the car wash every Saturday.

Around eight o'clock, the solitary ride, the first car, would roll in and park beside a vac-bot. There'd be a good jam on the stereo. Nothing loud, no need for excessive bass this early. The passenger side would be vacuumed first, then the floorboard, the seat, the back, then the driver's side. Soda-straw wrappers and six-day-old French fries would fly into the garbage can like dirt from a dog's hole. For breaks, this first Saturday Morning Car Wash Club member would look up and down the highway for cars he might recognize. Then back to work. Sweeping the crack where the seats folded forward, he would finally hear a beep-beep, and then another, and then a honk and a thump of bass. And for the next six hours he would go on cleaning and washing his car, watching the parade of incoming vehicles. As soon as the second Saturday Morning Car Wash Club member asked the first one for a quarter, the meeting officially commenced.

"Man, stop playin' around," I said, as the hooptie chugged closer and closer to the car wash. "You wanna get your ass beat this early?"

Chester had failed to tell me the whole truth about helping him wash his car. "Let's clean the machine," he'd said. I thought we were going to park it in his front yard and break out the water hose and the lemon-fresh Joy. I had no problem with that. What I did have a problem with was the fact that I was now riding in Chester's ugly brown rustmobile, his hooptie, his lemon, his clunker—in other words, his 1978 AMC Pacer.

I wasn't a big fan of the hooptie. Aside from the more obvious reasons for disliking Chester's ride, I charged the car with that most heinous variety of crime: a crime against childhood. Chester and I no longer watched cartoons. When the hooptie's first oil stains appeared on Chester's driveway our toon watching was over. Tools replaced the toons, motor oil replaced the milk in our Froot Loops, and the Bat Signal was answered by a super-inflated Michelin Man, hellbent on avenging bad front-end alignments. Chester's ugly brown rustmobile had killed Saturday morning cartoons forever, and it was about to kill us as well. We were heading toward the one place where ugly brown rustmobiles were chastised on a regular basis—the Saturday Morning "Back That Hunk of Junk Out of Here" Club. We were motorvating toward an early grave.

"Apollonia needs washin'," said Chester. "That's why I'm takin' her to the car wash. What's wrong with that?"

I jumped around beneath my seat belt. "What's wrong with that? Tommy, Buck, Mann, Leon. All of those fools hang out up there."

Chester strummed his fingers against the steering wheel; last week, he'd wrapped it with duct tape. He said it was for the grip, but I had never once seen Chester drive with anything more than a rotating palm.

"You're trippin'," he said, taking a wide right turn around a slow-moving car. "I'm grown. Everybody know me, everybody know you. It's the same fools at the car wash that be around the neighborhood." He turned and looked at me; I saw my reflection in his silver, mirrored shades. "You act like you're scared," he said.

"I ain't scared."

"You act like it."

The engine suddenly dropped, idled down, then shrieked back up three times louder. A fat little Vietnamese kid, playing in his front yard, picked up a stick and made as if to throw it at us. He ducked when the engine backfired.

"Do you know what they call this thing?" I asked.

"Apollonia," said Chester, stroking the dashboard.

"Doo-Doo Brown, man, they call your car Doo-Doo Brown. I was out at the pool yesterday, and as soon as I jumped in, everybody got out because they said they'd seen me riding around in the Doo-Doo-Mobile. What's up with that, man?"

Chester grinned. "That's all right, though. I see you ain't walkin' anywhere. Punks about fifty years old still ridin' the bus to school, ignorant. This is luxury."

I craned my head toward the roof of the car. Pockets of upholstery sagged down like small bellies against my face.

"I just don't feel like getting my ass beat this early, that's all," I said.

"Well, don't worry about it. Damn it." "Damn it" was the cuss of the moment. We'd been cussing since way back when, but the new thing that summer was to try to cuss like Eddie Murphy's father, or the way Eddie Murphy sounded when he impersonated his father—a drunken slur with attitude. Chester's Vernon was pretty good. Mine, on the other hand, sounded like me trying to sound like Chester trying to sound like Eddie Murphy trying to sound like his father.

"For real, though, man," said Chester. "This is where the ladies hang out."

"Oh yeah," I said. "The ladies."

"That's right. 'The ladies,'" said Chester. "But anyway, I know you don't want to walk up to the car wash with no car."

I thought about that for a second. The Saturday Morning Car Wash Club loomed just a few turns away from our current position. Apollonia's rattle was loud enough to be heard in Botswana. Meanwhile, there I was, afraid to put pressure against the passenger-side door for fear of tumbling out. Maybe walking wasn't such a bad idea.

"Doo-Doo Brown, huh?" said Chester, palming us into another turn. "We'll see what they call it when we ride off with all the sweet potatoes!" He laughed for a bit, and I would've laughed with him if he hadn't punched the speedometer in order to get the needle to move.

While Apollonia was revving herself into a fit, we slowly approached the hill between us and the car wash. Not a steep hill, if you were riding in anything other than a hooptie, but we were, of course, hooptienauts. Apollonia took to the incline like a pushcart on a roller-coaster track. When we finally crested the hill, I could see that the Saturday Morning Car Wash Club was already in session, at least it was until Apollonia backfired, frightening the members and a war-torn village or two somewhere in the Middle East. Chester looked at me. I looked at Chester. We rolled downhill in a prolonged, gear-grinding lurch.

"Luxury," I said.

"The ladies," said Chester. "Sweet potatoes! I told you they'd be here!"

If only my friend had taken off his shades and looked at his own reflection. There he was, practically kissing the windshield, grinning as we approached the car wash—and the ladies. Meanwhile, his right foot was hammering on the brakes, cheating Apollonia out of a sweet-potato massacre. The only thing more embarrassing than riding downhill in Chester's stalled car was riding downhill in Chester's stalled car toward every single girl that I'd ever planned on asking out. To this day, I firmly believe that Apollonia did more to steady the course of my virginity than my mother, my pastor, or those homemade Converse hightops that my cousin Meat Meat sold to me back in seventh grade. A true struggle buggy, a true hooptie, forms a clamp around the rider's crotch like some kind of pig-iron codpiece. I groaned as Apollonia shuddered to a halt.

"My hair look all right to you?" asked Chester.

It was barely nine o'clock, and already the Saturday Morning Car Wash Club was packed and vibrant. Not counting Apollonia, there were fifteen vehicles parked at various angles around the lot. Six of them sat inside the wash-and-wax bays. As usual, the guys who were washing their cars felt the need to go shirtless while they soaped. It didn't matter if they were muscular or not—something about a long black hose shooting chemically treated water urged them to work bare-topped. I could understand it if you were in your front yard with your toes in the grass, airing your car and the funk of your labor at the same time. But these jokers were flexing their pecs inside veritable saunas of industrial-strength detergent. You knew they were showing off for the benefit of the ladies, while the ladies were paying attention to anything but the soap operas. All that wax-o-wax and gunk-o-gunk repelled the females faster than drugstore-brand cologne. The guys never noticed. Most of them were too busy trying to scrape lovebugs off their headlights.

Six girls were at the car wash when Chester and I rolled in. Twice as many fellas were hovering around them. Most of these guys were older than we were, dropouts and two-time seniors, people who seemed to have owned rides all their lives. Some of the girls had their own cars. For the most part, they drove sporty, bright, quick-trip Civics, or Camrys, or whatever looked good behind an airbrushed vanity plate, and they brought them to the club for their boyfriends, or some other shirtless wonders, to give them a wash. Every one of these guys would treat his girlfriend's ride as if it were Cinderella's stagecoach. They'd use illicit waxes, controversial sponges, and forbidden emollients to rub, butter, and caress the various paint jobs. The only no-no was fooling around under the hood. The girls never allowed it. I don't know if it was Daddy's orders or suspicion of shade-tree mechanics, but rarely would you see a guy working on the engine of a girl's car. Their own cars, of course, they butchered no end.

"What's up, Chester?"

"Leon."

"What's up, Lorenzo?"

"Leon."

We'd barely got out of the car when Leon slid up with three of his *stank*-breath friends, all of them with towels around their necks soaking up the juice from their hairdos. Leon was already smirking.

"I like the ride, man," said Leon.

"Yep," said Chester.

"My sister got one just like it." Every time Leon opened his mouth, his boys would snicker. It was too early for an ass beating, and too hot. Leon was only three years older than us, but he'd been handing out ass beatings in Cedar Heights ever since I was old enough to walk to the playground by myself. I was tired of Leon. Maybe if somebody else had beaten my ass for a change, things would have been different, but Leon tended to bogart Cedar Heights ass like a demented Santa Claus who came every day except Christmas. He was a rusty-necked, two-toothed, head-cheese-eating bastard, and he always wore a mesh jersey with nothing underneath and thick gold-rope chains with foreign-car emblems hanging from them.

"Yeah, man, that's a smooth ride," said Leon. "What kind of gas you use?"

"I don't know," said Chester. "Gas."

Leon and his boys started laughing. I didn't get the joke. I looked over at Chester, and I could tell that he was becoming upset. The most vicious tool that the bad guys had was always their laughter. Leon had never uttered a funny phrase in his life, but he didn't really have to. His portable laughtrack took care of the rest.

I leaned back against Apollonia. Lime-green engine fluids fanned across the asphalt.

"Damn Doo-Doo Brown!" yelled Leon, affecting "the Vernon." "Doo-Doo Brown!"

Chester folded his arms. "I came here to wash my car, man, dang. Why ya'll always got to be messin' with people? Why don't you go worry about your own car?"

"Shoot, my car clean," said Leon, gesturing back to his black Camaro.

"I'm worried about Doo-Doo Brown. That junk start a rustquake, you gonna be washin' every car out here!"

He chortled. I knew what was coming before he could even say it, but he said it anyway. "I hate to tell you this, cuz, but your car is kinda messed up—for real, though. I ain't tryin' to be funny or nothin', but damn. It look like King Kong wiped his ass with a can of Pepsi. Look like a truckload of toe jam had an accident. Look like a roll of pennies with a damn steerin' wheel. I hate to tell you."

But, of course, he told us anyway. At one point or another, Leon compared Chester's car to a three-thousand-year-old foot, *stankin'* dried-up alligator balls, one roller skate being squeezed through somebody's ass, and two roller skates giving dried-up alligator balls a ride to the liquor store. Chester remained silent.

The more Leon and his boys laughed, the more attention they gathered. Music that had been pounding from the cars was turned down. Hoses were placed back on their hooks. Vacuums were switched off, and, most unfortunately, the girls drew near. No one had said the word "fight," but that's what everyone had heard, and that's what everyone expected. Leon had gained an audience. He'd hyped, he'd promoted, and he'd thoroughly teased; now all that was left was the main event.

"There ain't no room to wash that piece of doo-doo, no way," said Leon. "Why don't you ask your mama for a damn water hose, with those damn stupid shades. It look like you busted up a mirror to make that junk. *Ooh wee*, let me hold them shades, cool breeze!"

Before Leon raised his left hand to grab the sunglasses from Chester's face, I noticed two things about the crowd that had gathered around us. First, not everyone was amused by Leon's antics. Second, there was a girl standing off to the side whom I had not seen here before. Her name was Le Ly, and she was the one girl in the neighborhood that Chester always got quiet about whenever her name came up in conversation. She seemed out of place, but then again, I hardly ever saw her hanging out anywhere. When Leon raised his hand, I glimpsed her gazing at Chester. I intervened. With my right hand, I caught Leon's rising left.

"You better get yo' hand offa me!" roared Leon. "Walrus-lookin' punk, I'll punch you in yo' damn throat!"

My damn throat gulped. Holding his ashy wrist in my grip, I could feel the tendons wiggling into fist mode. "Do something!" the tendons were saying, wiring me like a traitor from within Leon's flesh. "Do something, man, don't just stand there feeling me up! This is the same fist that de-toothed the entire after-school chess program! Run! Run right now!"

"Race," I said, as Leon wrenched his hand free. "That messed-up hunk of rat turds you got can't beat this ride here. My man Chester says he'll race you for a spot."

"Shut up," said Leon. To my surprise, he stomped off toward the Camaro, boys in tow, towels dropped in their wake. I'd expected a punch or, at least, a smack. Foolish suggestions often drew smacks. With no smack to be had, the audience became a tense, buzzing mob of color commentators. "They crazy" was their main catchphrase.

"I know I didn't hear you say that," said Chester, turning to me with a frown. He removed his sunglasses and threw them inside the car. "Lorenzo, man, let's just go home."

"Why?" I asked. "Leon's already at home. Leon lives in Cedar Heights, too."

"Yeah, but—"

"Just get in the car, man." I opened the door and stood there until he got in. Making my way around the back of the car, I scanned the crowd for Le Ly. She had moved farther away, but her eyes were focussed on the hooptie.

"You'll thank me for this someday," I said, lowering myself into the seat. It took me a moment, while I slammed and re-slammed the door, to realize that Chester had placed his head on the steering wheel. He was crying.

"They're always messin' with me," he said, sobbing between gasps of air. "What did I do? They're supposed to be grown. How come grown folks always messin' with kids, man?"

I placed my hand on his shoulder. "Be cool," I said.

"Naw, bump that!" He raised his head up and faced the windshield. "Yeah, that's right, chumps!" he yelled, scowling at the onlookers, wiping snot on his sleeves. Leon's engine could be heard in the background. It sounded like an idling tractor: *Bow! Zugga zugga. Bow! Zugga zugga.*

"I can't race that fool," said Chester. "My mama will kill me if I wreck this car. My auntie gave me this car, man, I don't know what you're thinking about."

"Roll up your window," I said. "Nah, forget that. Just lean your car over."

"What?" asked Chester.

"Just listen, man. I think I know what to do."

It was the oldest trick in the book. With spectators on either side, both Leon and Chester revved their engines. They faced away from the car wash, toward the hill that led to it, the strip being the open road. I stood among the crowd, listening to the protests and disbelief. The general suspicion was that Chester was going to end up in the hospital.

"Let's get this mother gone!" yelled a friend of Leon's. A girl in a pair of pink hot pants stepped in between the two cars. Overhead, the blazing sun made jewels of the rocks in the asphalt. Apollonia seethed. Blue smoke billowed from every pipe.

"Dead man!" shouted Leon, leering from his dark ride.

"Ain't nothin' but a *thang*," said Chester, grinning behind the mirrored sky of his sunglasses. "Here come the sweet potatoes!"

The girl shrieked a countdown. Leon's car launched on "two," taking the hill and then vanishing in a thick fog of exhaust. People were still knocking the dust from their clothes when the first few giggles could be heard in Leon's wake.

"He calls that 'fast'?" said Chester, still sitting in the same position as before the countdown. "That's why his mama got sent to jail for stealin' hot sauce on Christmas."

The crowd had seen it coming. The six-day-old French fries had seen it coming. With the roar of the black Camaro receding in the distance, guffaws and loud talk arose from the spectators. "Told you!" they shouted to each other. "Told you!" and "Damn it!" and "I'll be dogged!" and, most vehemently, "Where my two dollars at?" Apollonia, whose engine was still running, slowly went into reverse, easing herself into the carwash bay made vacant by Leon's haste. Simply put, the hare had hauled tail and now the tortoise was taking up shack in the rabbit's hole. It was a Saturday morning cartoon. The Car Wash Club was hip, but not too hip for cartoons. They laughed and they cackled and they shook their heads. Even Leon's boys were making fun of his skid marks.

"What are we supposed to do when he comes back?" asked Chester, stepping out of the car.

"Pop the hatch," I said.

"Pop the hatch? What's that supposed to do?"

I smiled, glancing around to make sure Le Ly was still there. "It's supposed to open up the back, so I can get the cleaning stuff out. What's wrong with you, man? I thought we came here to wash Apollonia?"

"Oh, yeah," said Chester. A thousand words should have been pouring from my best friend's mouth. This was his hour. People were shaking his hand, but I knew who was really racing his heart.

"Nice sunglasses," she said, eying her own reflection.

Maile Chapman

A Love Transaction

From *Post Road*

It takes us hours to get everything cleaned up. I do the lighter jobs. He does the heavier jobs. He does anything with lifting, anything with twisting, anything that I can't do because I am prone to having cramps around the baby-thing. The entire area is sore, and lifting is bad, it provokes the pains down there. I have never told him about my health condition but I assume he must have guessed that I am not completely normal. I know he makes it easier for me, and in exchange I let him hurry me through. He has a standing plan for after work. It is probably a girl, I don't know, I almost don't want to know, I never ask and he never volunteers.

If he wants to know about it indirectly, he can find out from the office manager. She's the only one I've told, and I only tell her about my situation when it affects my job. Even then I don't tell her everything, not too many details. So far I have only told the minimum, that it pinches inside when I have to lift the metal gates and drag the hose out. I told her about the pressure from the baby-thing and the problems caused by the partial bones, because although they are small, and soft, it's uncomfortable when I have to bend down to do the gutters in the indoor runs.

We can have him do it for a while, she says. She seems sympathetic, but people don't really want to know the private story. I am sure it makes her want to go home and get away, get comfortable. She's got a husband.

That's what she says, she likes to go home on time so that she can see her husband. But sometimes she stays a few extra minutes to check in with us. With me, since he's usually already started on something. He doesn't talk at all during the first part of the shift. He sweeps, then turns on the waxer and guides it away from her, pretends he can't hear when she says it's time to have a word. So I listen. She tells me whether there are any overniters in the back, how many, what the special needs are. Someone puts a towel over their doors before we arrive so that we don't upset them with the equipment. We never even see them.

She slips on her belted raincoat while she goes over the details. She takes her purse out of the bottom drawer of the file cabinet, takes her keys off the hook. She wants to leave in her high-heeled shoes before the floors get wet. I have tried to get him to talk about her, I thought that maybe there was an attraction there, I thought maybe that's why she made the point to stay around a little, to see him, to try to talk to him over the hum of the waxer. When I brought it up he looked at me like I was crazy. Which was an answer that made me happy.

We have a pattern of activity together. While he does the indoor runs and the floor I go out back and dump the small boxes of waste. I take the outdoor broom to the fenced area and flip any stools into the bushes. After a while he comes out to smoke and I stand there a minute because he might say something, now that the worst part of the cleaning is over. Then I go inside to bleach the exam rooms and do a general wipe-down. When I'm almost done he gets on the phone. He has a conversation with someone, with whoever it is that waits for him every night. When he hangs up he says, are you almost finished? By then I am checking on the overniters. He won't have anything to do with that. He won't go near the berths, doesn't want to get that close. I put an ear to each, making sure I hear the breathing. We get ready to walk out the door together. He waits while I set the alarm, and then we're done.

Depending on his mood he will let me give him a ride somewhere. He likes to get out at a certain intersection midway between the clinic and where I live. He points and I pull over. At the intersection are a gas station, a tavern, and a dark apartment complex. He waits until I pull away before he starts walking. I'm sure he goes into the apartment complex. It is a poor-looking place. I think there's a girl in there, waiting. I know that he thinks I'm spoiled because I have the car. He doesn't understand the necessity. I can't do the walking that he does. I try to tell him this while we drive but I want to keep it vague. I always hope that when we talk he won't ask openly about my health. Saying too much about it would give the wrong impression, especially under the circumstances, he and I alone together in the darkness of the car.

I have appointments I need to get to, I say. I have to drive. I can't do the walking, for my medical reasons. I really can't.

He looks away out the window. He says, that's probably not any of my business.

I hope he won't make me say more. The best I can do is to think about my situation as hard as I can, and hope he picks up on it. I picture the proteins, the spotty tissues all sealed together. The baby-thing with hair and teeth comprising twenty percent of it. I think about how much I don't want to describe it to him just then. How much I want to be natural and not suggestive with my details. And he has mercy. I think he sees how it is with me. I think he knows that it isn't my fault, that it was a sterile happening, and that despite everything, I'm still a very nice girl. By this I mean that I have a good heart, and could be helpful. He could ask me for anything, and I'd give it to him.

The office manager waits and talks to me in private. First she asks about my health, and I tell her that none of the doctors is telling me anything new, that it's going to be surgery eventually. Even though I don't want to take the time off. She says that I can cross that bridge when I come to it. Then she asks how it's working out to have both he and I doing our shifts at the same time. I say that it works well. She asks whether it isn't too distracting and whether it isn't taking us too long to finish. Distracting? Did he say that? I am careful to be neutral. I ask her whether he has made any comments about me. Her kindness wavers and I see envy in her face. Not in so many words, she says. He's concerned with getting out on time.

We always get out on time, I say.

We'll talk again later, she says, getting ready to leave.

But I know that something is going on. He's been thinking it through on some level or he wouldn't have said anything about me, one way or another.

I stay out of his way, to make him wonder, to make him notice my absence when he goes out back to smoke. In the exam rooms I listen for him. I know that he is right there. I know that he is being careful not to think about me. My heart expands. The baby-thing shifts with excitement so that I have to stop and steady myself against the stainless steel table. I am almost sick with all of the possibility, all of the potential for happiness.

Nothing changes for several days, except that I avoid him. I find myself taking more time with the overniters. Adjusting the draping over the recovery area, repositioning the green mesh over the heatlamps.

Then I arrive and he is smoking outside in the parking lot. When I walk in he follows and goes into the back. The office manager is waiting. She says, he won't listen to me. Can you make sure that he knows there's a leak in the big room? He simply won't listen to me.

Runoff water is coming from somewhere. I can hear it hitting the floor.

She says, for god's sake get it mopped up.

The concrete walls are painted white. Water runs down them like glaze. I hear him turn on the waxer in the back.

He's going to be electrocuted, she says. I tell her that I will take care of the water. I promise. She wants to leave, and I want her to leave, to go home to her husband, to leave us alone.

When she is gone I bring towels from the utility room, dirty towels from the bin, I'm touching them with my bare hands but I don't care. The water slowly accumulates in the corners. I need more towels. Just leave it, he says. I'll do it.

There is a chill from the seeping water. I listen to the overniters and check the controls on all of their heating pads. I turn them each up by one setting. Not too much, otherwise the overniters who can't move will become dangerously overheated or even burned. Sometimes they are too weak to shift themselves off the pad. I hear him in the next room, moving towards the phone, making his usual call. I don't look under the

Maile Chapman

toweling but I can hear stirrings behind the bars when I pause outside each berth.

He is on the phone. He says, did you find out?

There is nothing but the sound of water, and then he says, I don't believe it.

There are jerky movements in the last recovery berth, the sound of nails against stainless steel. I move the toweling a little. I make larger movements than necessary, to catch his eye and remind him that I am here but he doesn't notice. He stares straight down at the phone. He says, are you sure? His voice gets lower; are you sure? Okay, he says finally. Okay, but stop. If you're sure then crying won't help now. He hangs up. I repeatedly adjust the toweling. It is light pink, frayed around the edges. I tuck it more securely around the frame of the door.

I keep my back to him. I am giving him the chance to make up his mind about something. My fingers are between the bars for a long moment during which I hear nothing from him in the room behind me. I try to maintain my calm. I hear the nails again faintly and I am afraid that the overniter is about to touch my fingers. Maybe bite my fingers. But I know they are all delirious, not even aware of me.

He pulls the waxer away from the wall. Pauses.

Can you give me a ride somewhere? he says. It is the first time he has had to ask.

Of course, I say. Inside I feel a mounting pressure. I slide my fingers further into the cage. Labored breathing. Delirium.

He puts the equipment away, the floors undone. He lines the corners and baseboards with rags to catch the seepage. He is on his knees.

I do the exam rooms, fast. He is waiting. He is nervous. He can't stand still and goes outside. I step out of the building, lock the door. Set the alarm. Push the buttons. He throws his cigarette into the gravel and we get into the car.

I drive him to a cash machine where he withdraws the maximum allowed. Then he asks me to take him to another cash machine nearby, where he attempts to make another withdrawal. He has reached his daily limit. He reads the screen, appears not to understand. He tries again but can't take out any money. He gets back into the car, waits, and then asks me to drive him to another cash machine.

By now it is dark out. I tell him it's no use, that no machine will let him take more. He says he has to keep trying. He won't look at me. I know he is thinking that I don't understand, that I can't understand the frustration.

How much? I say.

His hand twitches on his leg.

I don't know, he says. Anything.

I step out of the car with my purse, take out my debit card. It slides neatly into the machine. My fingers feel swollen when I press the numbers. I know what kind of gesture this is. I would take it all out, if it weren't for the limit, and so I go that far, and will give it to him in crisp new bills. I get back into the car and sit beside him. Breathless. My hand touches his when he takes the money. His eyes look shiny and red. I feel a pulsing everywhere, a throbbing even in my throat, because now I know that eventually I will have him. Now I know that the girl in the apartment complex will be easy enough to forget, it will only take money to fix that situation. And I never even had to bring up the baby-thing. All of that has been left undescribed—there is still all of the telling to look forward to. I'm thinking about the patience he will have to have, and the secret things he will do for me when we are alone together in a safe place. I have to sit and hold it in for a second before I can drive, before I can even turn the key, because of the movement, the excitement, the hidden cartilage twisting in anticipation of him.

Maile Chapman

Pedro Ponce

The Revelation Museum

From *Alaska Quarterly Review*

In the Revelation Museum, we will lie on wooden pallets and look up through rented binoculars at pictures of the future. You will marvel at the Millennial Tapestry, at the embroidered dragon shown nesting in the remains of the earth. You will part your lips and arch your back at things that are yet to be. Through my smudged plastic eyepiece, I will see the shower-damp strands tucked behind your ear, the slice of tanned skin exposed by your shifting hips, the train ticket peering from the pocket of your handbag.

In the future, movies will consist entirely of previews. There will be all the sweep of a promising beginning with none of the sad sobriety that comes from ending, the soft drink traces that sour the tongue, the slow shuffle toward the exits, the manufactured daylight that rouses the audience home.

We will wander through familiar exhibits: The City of Tomorrow. Fashions of the Future. In the Hall of Prophets, you will say that I don't have to.
　Don't have to what?
　Follow me. Out. Just leave me at the gate.
　We will stand before the wax figure of a bearded man wearing purple

robes. I will stare at the astrolabe he wields behind thick protective glass, ignore the glass-mirrored image of your profile turned toward me. I will remain mute and standing as grade school tour groups overtake us, as you unlace your fingers from mine and walk away.

Psychic stalkers will terrorize America. They will elude authorities and confound the courts. The lovelorn, lacking paranormal foresight, will employ them illicitly for surveillance work, consoled in the knowledge that the objects of their longing are always predictably within reach.

The hall that houses the Giant Clock will grow vacant in the waning afternoon. Solitary visitors will linger along the minute track and contemplate their warped reflections in the steep brass bezel. From the terrace of the Cafe Nostradamus, we will watch as tourists gather at the center of the clock face. Some will look through the transparent semicircle beneath their feet and, ignoring posted warnings, take pictures of the exposed wheels and springs. Others will look up at the hour and minute hands as they make their slow progress above the thinning crowd.

I will raise an old argument: What does a consultant do, anyway, and why must they do whatever they do in such a distant city?

You will smile. As you fold and unfold an empty sugar packet, you will explain about markets, projections, polls. You will mention your larger apartment and the inexpensive airfare there and back.

I will not be listening. I will be looking down at the hands of the Giant Clock. They will stretch in a nearly straight line over the crowd below. The shadows they cast will grow broad in the dimming daylight, dark wings veiling the faces of the young and old.

In my best dreams, you won't be naked. You will be leaning close against me, your breath teasing the crook of my neck. I will feel my hand in the easy grip of your fingers, your body cleaved to mine in an unbroken stillness.

As we stand before the Posterity Capsule, I will see you check your watch. You will see me see you, then you will look down to read the exhibit placard. It will invite us to contribute to the capsule's contents, which will be buried on Museum property and excavated after five thousand years. On seeing the crammed bottom half of the open capsule, you will ask, What more do they need?

Grabbing the ticket from your handbag, I will say that no time capsule is complete without a souvenir of ancient transportation systems. You will try and fail to look serious as you ask for the ticket back. I will have only meant to dangle it over the capsule's edge, but I will find myself digging deep beneath layers of letters, snapshots, and pocket New Testaments, until I am pressing the ticket flat against the cool metal bottom.

Your shouts will attract Museum security and the irritation of passers-by. One of the officers will ask if there is a problem. I will withdraw my arm without answering.

I will wait until I know you are seated before going out to the platform. Straggling passengers will rush toward the last open cars, their luggage swinging heavily from hands and shoulders. I will think I see you in one of the train's tinted windows, think I recognize your profile sipping water from a bottle. I will watch the window closely until the train begins to pull out, until I can't tell which one of us is really moving.

In the neighborhood grocer's, I will handle packaged meat and lettuce heads, cereal boxes and dented cans. I will return my basket, unfilled, to one of the narrow check-out aisles. The familiar smell of cheap newsprint will stop me and for the rest of the night, I will find distraction in the weekly news of the world:

Medical Experts Confirm:
> *Too Much Sex May Be Bad For You!*
Second Noah's Ark Set to Launch!
> *. . . Will You Be Onboard?*
Resurrect the Dead in Ten Easy Steps:
> *Georgia Minister Shows How!*

September will bring rain spots to the windowsill, strange hairs lingering in unturned sheets, the corpse of a moth clinging to a bed of dust.

*

We will trade the day's events by phone. I will ignore the awkward pauses that break up our conversation, the way your voice grows more distant the longer we talk. You will send me kisses before hanging up, but through the static of a bad connection they will grate my ears like the drone of an alarm clock.

In the Revelation Museum, I will stand alone between howling infants and dozing travelers to view the wonders of the Virtual Community. Two adjacent displays—one marked "Los Angeles," the other "New York"—will portray simultaneous social functions. In Los Angeles, mannequins in shorts and shirtsleeves will share drinks on a sunlit patio. In New York, revelers will hunch avidly over a board game. Over the border between displays, two figures will face each other wearing thickly visored helmets. Holding empty champagne glasses, they will raise a toast across a simulated continent.

There will be consultants in every home. They will use market research and demographics to determine dinner menus, argument outcomes, schedules for intercourse. They will survey neighbors on the curbing of noise pollution and the upkeep of lawns. They will quiz near and distant relatives for topics to avoid during holiday visits. If numbers fall below a predetermined level, they will have the power to dissolve partnerships, bolstered by pie charts, graphs, and quarterly reports.

She will be close enough. She will be attractive enough. She will be willing enough. She will sleep through my sleeplessness, curling indifferently around the space I leave behind in bed. I will not return until daylight glazes the tops of trees and the chill of morning sends me shivering back for the nearest warmth.

I will attend too many weddings, too often unaccompanied. I will be trapped in too many conversations about the bride's beauty, the groom's charm. In hotel reception halls, I will drain watery cocktails as couples descend to the dance floor. Bob Marley will sing to the solitary and spoken for: *Everything is gonna be alright.* Later, nursing the beginnings of a hangover, I will think: *But nothing is gonna be great.*

Pedro Ponce

Government officials will be elected by beauty pageant. Celebrity judges will consider candidates based on interviews, special talents, and appearances in evening wear. To preserve national morale, the swimsuit competition will be eliminated.

Romantic attachments will be determined by popular vote. The attractive and eligible will debate each other and make their cases on daytime television. Those candidates who cannot afford a viable campaign will be sent home with door prizes and encouraged to swell the diminishing ranks of the clergy.

You will meet him through a friend. You will meet him by accident. He will be merging businesses, writing the great American novel, fighting for the people. He will be teaching the poor children of the world how to fight for the people, how to write the great American novel, how to merge their own businesses. His appearance will promise you beautiful Teutonic babies. His fucking will be an epic that begins without the need for muses. He will lurk behind the pauses when we speak, the receiver cold in your hands, your voice betraying nothing.

You will not age well. In the golden years of your marriage, your husband will wake up next to your sagging body, your crusted mouth, the stench of your incontinence. He will shut his eyes, turn away, and think the thoughts of an aging Romeo, longing for the dagger that could have stabbed you both into everlasting love.

I will forget you easily. Only my hands will remember. They will seek you at the periphery of daily routine. They will feel your wrist in the handle of a brief case, your mouth in the tug of a wet dishcloth, the rise and fall of your breathing in the cold smoothness of new bedding.

It will be discovered that the world is the delusion of a street-corner psychopath. His unmedicated hallucinations will be exposed as the source of all reality. An international debate will ensue: Should treatment be risked at the expense of the world as we know it? After months of discussion, doctors will hazard a moderate dose of Librium. This will free the masses from junk mail, the common cold, and jury duty. The public's favor will last until a dose of Compazine does away with cable television. There will be riots, protests, all too late. Curiosity will get the better of the scientific community as treatment continues. Xanax will take out the environment. Risperdal will dismantle the economic infrastructure. Men of the cloth will globally decry the waste of life and resources until Thorazine takes care of them and their churches. The earth will grow flat and barren until an overdose of Stelazine eliminates the scientific community. Released from medical scrutiny, the patient will preside over what remains of the populace, haunted by those delusions too stubborn for treatment: progress, coherence, posterity, destiny.

Foresight is a fiction. We are merely predictable. The future is visible to any open eye. It waits in the empty luggage at the foot of the bed, in the moth that crawls on the windowsill, in the tick of a second hand in the blue light of morning, in the slope of your bare shoulders sighing with sleep.

I will not follow you out. I will leave you at the gate. I will make my way out of the station and wait by the deserted taxi rank. Across the broad boulevard, the marble angel that guards the Revelation Museum will put its lips to a gold trumpet. I will listen for the noise of movement behind me, knowing that you are already lost, even before the track lights begin to blink, even before your train creeps out under the void of a new moon.

Pedro Ponce

T . E . H o l t

Ὁ Λογος

From *Zoetrope*

The first case of which any record survives was reported in a small town daily in upstate New York. Tabitha Van Order, the brief item reads, age five, was brought into the county hospital's emergency room with "strange markings" on her face and hands. "She was playing with the newspaper," her mother reported. "I thought it was just the ink rubbed off on her." But the marks did not respond to soap or turpentine. At the hospital, initial examination determined that the marks were subcutaneous, and the child was admitted for observation. They looked, according to the triage nurse, as though someone had been striking the child with a large rubber stamp. "They look like bruises," the emergency-room physician told the *Journal* reporter. The department of social services was looking into the case.

This alone might not have warranted even three inches on page 8 of a sixteen-page paper. What attracted the attention of the editor at the county desk (whose sister, a nurse in the E.R., had phoned in the story), and earned Tabitha's case even that scanty initial notice, was one peculiar feature of those bruises, one fact about the case that stood out from the face of an otherwise unremarkable, seemingly healthy little girl. It was not that, over the next several days, the marks did not fade, nor exhibit any of the changes of hue or outline usual in a bruise—although this was puzzling. Nor was it the child's silence, which she maintained three days with a patient gravity that impressed the most casual of observers. What claimed the attention of everyone who saw the child over the three days of her illness was the unmistakable pattern in those marks. They formed a word.

A word, certainly: no one who saw doubted for an instant what they saw. And it was something more, as well. Everyone struck with the sight of that pale, silent face and that black sign reported the same response: each said that the shock of seeing it for the first time was almost physical. It was as if, the nurse on the day shift recalled, seeing it, you felt it on your own face—"like a blush." And indeed, after the initial shock, something like embarrassment did set in: the nurses could never bring themselves to utter the word, either to the child or among themselves; the physicians during their morning rounds half averted their eyes even as they palpated the affected areas. And although *bruises* were discussed day and night across the desk at the nursing station; although *palpable purpura* were the subject of long discussions in the cafeteria; although everyone down to the orderlies hazarded a guess as to the nature of the *marks*, the *word* itself went euphemized, persistently elided.

After embarrassment followed another response, something of which communicates itself even now in the tone of that first newspaper article, a kind of delicacy, a reticence over the details of the case: a hush. That respectful silence grows ambivalently louder in the two pieces that in as many days followed, lengthened, and moved forward toward page one. As for the child herself, she made no complaint, nor in fact did she utter any word at all until just before the end, when she was heard to pronounce, in tones audible as far as the nursing station, the word spelled out by the bruise across her hands, cheeks, jaw, and (most plainly) forehead. She spoke the word in a piercing falsetto three times, and then, before the nurse could reach the room, the child coded, as the physician's assistant said, and died.

I learned much of this, of course, later, by which time several of the principals—the nurses, the orderlies, the mother, and the physicians—were beyond the reach of my own inquiries. But I believe the editor told me as much of the truth as he knew before he died.

Which was more than he told his readers. Even in the third article, which appeared on the fourth day following Tabitha's admission to the hospital, and where the headline type has grown to fifty-four points, the text is most significant for what it does not say. It does not tell the precise form of those bruises that darkened across the child's features in her last twelve hours and then faded completely within minutes of her death— although the darkening and the fading both are faithfully set down. Nor does it transcribe the syllables the child voiced three times before she died—although the fact of her crying out is also given. It does not even mention that the bruises formed a word.

There was this aspect of the affair notable from the start: that embarrassment that overcame all who saw the word, as if the thing were shameful. Not, I believe, for what it said, but for being so patently, inscrutably significant: for being *a sign*. Few people could bring themselves, at first, even to acknowledge what they saw. It was as if an angel had planted one bare foot in Central Park, another on the Battery, and cast the shadow of a brazen horn over Newark. If such had happened, how many minutes might we suppose to have elapsed before anyone could have brought himself to turn to his neighbor and ask: Do you see? How could any of us discuss it without feeling implicated? So it was in the case of Tabitha's word: it was too plainly part of a world we no longer knew how to address.

But there was more to this evasion, of course, than met the eye, and it is this that I find truly remarkable about the case. It is the function of that evasion, and the unmistakable conclusion it urges, that most impresses me: that everyone who saw the word, immediately, *without* understanding, without conscious thought or any evidence at all, knew that to see the word in print was a sentence of death.

No one, at the time, had any empirical reason for suspecting such, but in every account, even the first, I trace an instinctive recognition that the word carried the contagion. It was several months, of course, before the means of transmission was identified, through the work of the Centers for Disease Control and Prevention in Atlanta and Lucerne, and ultimately the heroic sacrifice of the interdisciplinary team at the École des Hautes Études en Sciènces Sociales in Paris. So how do we find, in this first written record, the prudence that spared until a later date so many lives? And how do we balance that seeming prudence with the other inescapable fact about the word: that as the end approached, all seemed seized—as was Tabitha herself—with an impulse to speak it. It was as if the word struggled to speak *itself*, as if in answer to some drive to propagate that would not be denied.

The elucidation of the mechanism was complicated by the discovery that mere speech was harmless, as was hearing: it was the eye through which the plague entered, and the eye only. The hand that wrote, so long as the person behind it did not look, was spared (with the notorious exception of the blind, who took the illness in Braille, and broke out before they died in portentous boils). But to see the word in print (ink or video, it did not matter) was to sicken, and invariably to die.

Experimental studies were hampered, of course, by a number of complicating factors, not least of which was the obvious difficulty in conducting tests on other than human subjects. A late attempt was made, by some accounts, to incorporate the word into the ideogrammatic code taught to chimpanzees at the Yerkes Center for Primatology; results were fragmentary, the experiment ending prematurely with the incapacitation of the staff. One significant datum did emerge from all studies, however: illiteracy was no defense. Even those incapable of deciphering the dialogue from comic strips were found to be susceptible. The only exceptions were those functioning, for whatever reason, below the mental age of thirty months.

But all of this knowledge came later. Although this most important aspect of the disease did ultimately receive full measure of publicity, in the case of Tabitha Van Order the initial reports were mute. Indeed, were it not owing to the early curiosity of one researcher in virology at a nearby university, the epidemiological particulars of this first case might have passed almost entirely unrecorded. This virologist, one Taylor Salomon, happened to have been a patient on the same floor as the child, incapacitated with pneumonia, which she had contracted while at work in her laboratory. On the day that Tabitha gave up the ghost in a room four doors down from hers, Professor Salomon was sitting up in bed for the first time in two weeks, taking some clear broth and attempting to organize notes from her research.

T. E. Holt

The attempt was futile, owing to the extreme weakness that had kept her semiconscious for the previous two weeks, and was disrupted forever by the unearthly cry that heralded Tabitha's demise. Professor Salomon was fortunate in this, however: her own illness had kept her from visiting the child's room, or even glimpsing her mottled face through the open door, before the marks had faded entirely away. And the research project that had hospitalized Professor Salomon soon faded from her thoughts as well, supplanted by a new question as soon as the nurse appeared, visibly shaken, in answer to the professor's call.

The nurse could relate the sequel of the child's cry, but not its meaning; she could only echo, with the distracted air that had come to typify the medical staff in the last hours of Tabitha's life, the helpless distress of her colleagues at finding their patient so unaccountably dead. To Salomon's more pertinent questions about the disease's course and etiology, the nurse could only wring her hands and look back over her shoulder, as if she harbored a guilty secret. Her curiosity piqued, Professor Salomon managed to rise from her bed and stumble down the hall before the orderlies arrived to wheel the body away. The marks had apparently disappeared no more than five minutes before her arrival.

Luck was with her again, in that her appearance in the room was followed almost immediately by that of the medical examiner. The examiner, already irritated at the interruption of lunch, was inclined to order Salomon from the room, and her recitation of her credentials did nothing, at first, to soothe him. But being in no mood to take up the investigation himself, his irritation was no match for Salomon's persistence, and in the end he agreed to provide the samples she required. In an additional example of the good fortune that marked so much of Salomon's involvement with the case, the M. E.'s cooperative attitude was not shared by the hospital staff, which refused to release the child's chart to anyone but the M. E., citing doctor-patient confidentiality. But the samples, Salomon felt, would prove more valuable than any M.D.'s scribble, and she was content with the oral recitation of the child's history she eventually wrung from the nurses. The samples, iced and isolated according to protocols, waited another two weeks before Salomon was able to return to her lab, where she found, of course, nothing. The blood, nerve tissue, and other fragments of Tabitha's clay were apparently those of a healthy five-year-old girl, and nothing an extremely well-funded laboratory could bring to bear on them was able to add anything to the story.

Stymied in the laboratory, Salomon turned to a colleague in epidemiology, and, swearing him to secrecy, initiated field studies of the child's home, school, and other haunts. The season was late spring; the child's backyard abutted on a swamp: insect traps were set and their prey examined (at this point the impromptu task force expanded to include an entomologist). Once again, nothing significant appeared.

Time was running out for Salomon and her hope of scoring a coup. Five weeks after Tabitha's admission to the hospital, the child's mother, the triage nurse, four orderlies, the emergency-room physician's assistant, three floor nurses, and two doctors were admitted with livid bruises on the palms of their hands, cheeks, jaws, and (most plainly) foreheads.

In this first wave of cases, the disease exhibited additional symptoms, not observed (or not reported) in the case of Tabitha Van Order. In the triage nurse, onset was marked by a vague dreaminess that overtook her at work one morning. By lunchtime, she was incapable of entering insurance information correctly on her forms, and by midafternoon she had wandered from her desk. She was found on one of the high floors of the hospital, staring out a window at the lake, where a sailboat regatta was in progress. It was only at this point that the marks on her face were noticed. At about this time (the precise time is unavailable, owing to the nurse's absence from her desk), Julia Van Order arrived at the emergency room, brought in by a neighbor who had found her laughing uncontrollably in the street outside her home. The third symptom, glossolalia, was observed in two of the orderlies and one physician, who were admitted over the course of the evening. By midnight, there were twelve patients on the floor.

Recognizing an incipient epidemic, the chief of infectious disease imposed strict quarantine that evening. Staff on the floor were issued the customary isolation gear, and strict contact precautions were imposed. Who could blame the man for not issuing blindfolds? Such measures were in fact tried, much later, but by then, of course, it was much too late. He failed as well to confiscate pens.

Professor Salomon, on hearing of these new admissions, realized that

T.E. Holt

her time was running out, and did the only thing left to her. After one visit to the hospital, during which she conducted interviews with those of the victims able to respond, she wrote up as full a description of the disease as she could, took her best guess (which turned out, in the end, to be wrong) as to its cause, sealed the four typewritten pages in a dated envelope, and sent the sealed article, with a cover letter, to *The New England Journal of Medicine*. It was not at that time the policy of the *New England Journal* to accept so-called *plis cachetés*, the practice having fallen into disrepute over a generation earlier, and Salomon's contribution might have been returned unopened had it not been for yet another fortuitous circumstance.

A reporter specializing in science and medicine was visiting Salomon's university that week, lecturing graduate students in journalism. On the day he was scheduled to return to New York, he happened to hear of the dozen deaths that had occurred the previous night at the county hospital. Sensing a career opportunity, he filed a story, complete with an interview with Salomon, and the item ran prominently in the Health section of the following week's issue.

The reporter, who had conducted his interviews with the hospital staff over the phone, and filed in the same way, was fortunate. Professor Salomon was not; time had in fact run out for her in more ways than one. Before she died, however, she had the satisfaction of seeing her report in print, its publication in the *New England Journal* spurred on by the article in *Time*.

In the four weeks that followed the first wave, mortality in the county was misleadingly low. The local daily never having printed the word, the contagion was spread almost exclusively among the hospital staff, in whom the disease lay latent for the month of July. At the end of the first week of August, the marks broke out over the hands, cheeks, jaws, and (most prominently) foreheads of approximately eighty-five doctors, nurses, orderlies, speech therapists, and social workers, most of whom were brought in by their families in various stages of confusion, euphoria, and glossolalia.

In this second wave, observers reported yet another symptom, which followed those exhibited in the first wave in a distinct progression. Whether the onset was marked by dreamy confusion, giddiness, or fluently unintelligible speech, within twelve hours all such symptoms had lapsed into one: an uncontrollable paranoia, in which the sufferer was convinced that every object in the world, animate or inanimate, was involved in a vast conspiracy to do the patient harm.

Without exception, in this stage of the disease its victims spoke continuously for periods of up to twenty-four hours, offering elaborately detailed descriptions of the delusional system in which they were enmeshed. And without exception, the attending physicians reported that they had at times to fight off the conviction that their patients' dreams were real. Who can blame them? Confronted with an undeniable health emergency, swift to spread, invariably fatal, and marked at its heart by the inscrutable symbol of the word, little wonder that those who struggled to understand the disease struggled as well with fear. Unlike their patients, who had evolved an explanation for the menace within them, their doctors had no such comfort, and could only watch their patients die, and wonder helplessly if they had contracted the plague as well.

For plague, by the end of the first week of September, it had become. There is little point in going over the statistics of that hellish week: the figures beggar comprehension, and mere repetition will not suffice to make them meaningful. Certainly their import was dulled by the more immediate, personal tragedies that struck almost every household in the country at that time. And as the numbers grew to embrace other nations, other languages, their meaning became in no way more intelligible. No more than did the word, which, as it appeared in different nations, took on different forms, but everywhere with the same effect.

At this time, little remains to report, but I would like to offer before I close two or three items that strike me as significant. The first, as I have hinted, was almost lost in the events that followed so quickly on the disease's emergence into the public eye. But Professor Salomon's team, in the weeks between her death and theirs, continued its research into the origins of the contagion. And though the trail had by then grown cold, the scent was not so faint that they could find in this an excuse for the failure of their investigations: the disease was untraceable, they claimed, because *it had no physical cause.*

And here I find one of the most pathetic effects of this disease—the

T. E. Holt

kind of case in which its action was so grievous because so clearly marked. One of Salomon's survivors, a geneticist, whom I had known slightly during our years together at the university, and who was one of the few men I have ever met who might have deserved to be called a genius, telephoned me on the day the disease took hold of him. While I kept him on the phone, in the thirty minutes before help arrived, I listened as he spun out the delusion that had come on him with the word. The spectacle, if I may call it that, of a mind of his caliber reduced to raving brought me close to tears.

But I feel obligated to report what he said to me that day, in part because it was my only immediate contact with a victim of the plague. And also because one aspect of the encounter still strikes me, somehow, as significant. *I believed.* All the time I was speaking to him, I found myself fighting off conviction. Naturally, the feeling passed, but I still find myself, several weeks later, struggling with a sense of opportunity missed: I felt at the time, and still in my weaker moments do, as though I had come close to penetrating the mystery of the word. This is, of course, one of the effects most frequently reported by those attending on the dying.

The disease, my caller insisted, was not, properly speaking, a plague. That is to say, it was not spread by any of the infectious mechanisms. The word was not a pathogen: it was a *catalyst*, and the disease itself immanent in humanity at large. He had deciphered a sequence, he claimed, in the human genome, which matched, in the repetitive arrangement of its amino acids, the structure of the word. It seemed the word, processed in the temporal lobe in the presence of sufficient quantities of norepinephrine—the quantities released at levels of anxiety commonly associated with fear of bodily harm—acted as a trigger for this hitherto unnoticed gene. The gene, once stimulated, distorted the chemical function of the cerebral cortex, and the result was the familiar progression of stigmata, hallucination, convulsion, death.

It was, of course, palpable nonsense. I did not tell him so. Pity restrained me. He needed me, he went on, to spread the word. I chided him, gently, on his phraseology. His response was impatient to the point of fury. I had to help, he insisted: my own expertise in linguistics dovetailed so neatly with his findings. The two of us, he said, could broadcast the key needed to unlock a cure. I allowed him to speak as long as he needed to, until the ambulance arrived and the receiver was quietly set down. Triage, in those days, was performed upon the spot.

The man's ravings were, of course, merely one more instance of the paranoia that marks the final hours of the victims of the plague. But, like all paranoid fantasies, his had some germ of truth in them, and it tantalized me. If we accept that the disease came into this world without phenomenal cause, another possibility remains. The disease is, I grant, born in the brain. But it is not the product of any mechanism so vulgar as genetic coding. It is purely a product of the human mind.

I offer this as a message of hope. For if the plague had its origins in the human mind, might it not be fought by the same powers that called it forth? Tabitha had been "playing with the newspapers," her mother reported. So, this night, have I. I have before me the pages, already growing yellow, of the *I———— Journal* in the first weeks of June. I visited the newspaper's offices last night, forced to break in with a wrecking bar. The streets of the town were still, but for someone singing in the upper floor above a nearby shop. The words of the song were unintelligible: only the tune came through, a wandering melody, almost familiar.

I have spread them out here before me, these pages from the morgue, my fingers trembling, the paper brittle, my breath unsteady in my chest. I read the stories there: they are the old familiar ones, always the same. Family burned in a fire. Two held in convenience-store murder. Ultimatum issued over Balkan genocide. Plague in the Middle East. Old news. These portents and omens reduced to columns of fading ink.

I know, of course, the risk I am taking. I know only too well how fragile has been the chain of circumstances that has protected me from the infection. I listen even now to the stillness outside my window and am awed by the hush there, and what it says to me of my own great fortune. It is a mournful silence, broken only by the eternal singing of the katydids. They call, as they always have, of the coming of winter: mournful, and yet somehow pleasant, as all melancholy is.

But before I digress again, I would report the last significant item I have in my possession, and then I must go back to my own work, which has been too long interrupted. The information is this. In the later stages of the plague, the word disappeared. Almost as if it were no longer necessary, the last victims sickened, raved, and died without any visible sign of illness. I have a theory, of course. And although there is no means at my disposal to prove it even to my own satisfaction, I am convinced it is true.

The word, whatever it meant, whatever form it took in whatever language, was not the carrier of plague: not in any of the ways we sought to *understand.* Understanding was beside the point: for how could Tabitha, herself illiterate, have understood? The answer, plainly, is that she did not. I can imagine the scene vividly, even now, as the child turned the pages of the newspaper, rehearsing in her thoughts such anxieties as she had heard adults around her voice over pages such as these. Anxieties she did not understand, yet could not help but share: anxieties that, for all she knew, were made of words. Words she could not understand, but still she searched among them for some clue, some answer to the riddle of her life.

Children are suggestible, reader. To go from fear of unintelligible danger to a physical expression of that fear required only one word, any word, any arbitrary sequence of letters that happened to come to her as she "read." That word, written in blood on her features, took her to the hospital, confirming all her fears—fears that conspired, after three days and nights of what must have been pure, unremitting terror, to stop her heart.

Do you doubt me, reader? What more would you have? Letters of fire across the sky? A voice speaking prophecy in your sleep? A look in the mirror at your own forehead? A list, perhaps, of the ways death can come to you, even as you read here, safe in your home?

What is it you want? The word?

I give you this, and then I must be gone. All you need is here before you—and the knowledge that what kills us now is any word at all, read in the belief that words can kill.

I know this now. I have been convinced for several days.

ʼΟ Λογος

ʼΟ Λογος

ʼΟ Λογος

Patrick A. Rosal

Following My Year-Long Absence

From *The Literary Review*

Another morning's snared over the Raritan.
The Lenten rain's
                    stalled in a cumulus of fume.
Transit cars scan their cables suspended
like the catenary arms of thieves. And, Father,

what I'm saying is I can't say
you and I have loved each other bravely.
And I can't tell you this has changed.

You see, there is a God between us
hanging like a metal spike
and each time I lean to kiss you it begins to swing.

Isn't this the same God who
let there be water and let there be light

Father, I'm nearly
                    the man you wanted as a son.
I'm learning to tell you what I can't say.
Turn to me and see—an unfinished man
on the verge of silence, on the verge of saying.

Lucille Clifton

Lazarus

From *Callaloo*

first day

i rise from stiffening
into a pin of light
and a voice calling
"Lazarus, this way"
and i walk or rather
swim in a river of sound
toward what seems to be
forever   i am almost
almost there when i hear
behind me
"Lazarus, come forth" and
i find myself swiveling
in the light for this
is the miracle Mary Martha,
at my head and at my feet
singing my name
is the same voice

second day

i am not the same man
borne into the crypt.

as ones return from otherwhere
altered by what they have seen,

so have i been forever.

lazarus.
lazarus is dead.

what entered the light was one man
what walked out is another.

third day

on the third day i remember
what i was moving from
what i was moving toward

light again and
i could feel the seeds
turning in the grass   mary
martha i could feel the world

now i sit here on a crevice
in this rock   stared at
answering questions

sisters stand away
from the door to my grave
the only peace i know

Agha Shahid Ali was educated at the University of Kashmir, Srinagar, and University of Delhi. He earned a Ph.D. in English from Pennsylvania State University and an MFA from the University of Arizona. His volumes of poetry include *The Country Without a Post Office, Bone Sculpture, A Nostalgist's Map of America,* and *The Beloved Witness: Selected Poems.* He is also the translator of *The Rebel's Silhouette: Selected Poems,* by Faiz Ahmed Faiz. Mr. Ali has received fellowships from The Pennsylvania Council on the Arts, the Bread Loaf Writers' Conference, the New York Foundation for the Arts, and the Guggenheim Foundation. He is currently on leave from the University of Massachusetts, Amherst.

Josefina Báez is an author, actress, and educator who works in multidisciplinary and multicultural context and intercultural in scope. She has participated in many theater festivals and workshops around the world and was a fellow artist in the 2000 Asian Pacific Performance Exchange Program at UCLA. She has taught theater and creative writing in the New York City public schools since 1984 and is a faculty member of Creative Arts Laboratory at Teachers College, Columbia University.

Maile Chapman's fiction has appeared or is forthcoming in *LIT,* the *St. Ann's Review,* and the *Denver Quarterly.* She is currently a Fulbright Grantee living in Finland.

Lucille Clifton has published numerous books since 1969, when her first book of poetry was named one of the year's ten best books by the *New York Times.* Her later poetry collections include *Quilting: Poems 1987–1990* and *The Terrible Stories*. She has also written prose pieces, including *Generations: A Memoir* and *Memoir: 1969–1980*. Her many children's books written expressly for an African-American audience include *All Us Come Cross the Water*, *My Friend Jacob*, and *Three Wishes*. She received creative writing fellowships from the National Endowment for the Arts in 1970 and 1973, and a grant from the American Academy of Poets. She has received the Shelley Memorial Prize, the Charity Randall prize, the Shestack Prize from the *American Poetry Review*, and an Emmy Award. In 1988, she became the first author to have two books of poetry chosen as finalists for the Pulitzer Prize (*Good Woman: Poetry* and *Next: New Poems*). She is a Distinguished Professor of Humanities at St. Mary's College of Maryland.

Edwidge Danticat received a degree in French literature from Barnard College and an MFA in writing from Brown University. Recipient of a James Michener Fellowship, she is the author of two novels, *Breath, Eyes, Memory* and *The Farming of Bones*, and a collection of short stories, *Krik? Krak!*, a National Book Award finalist. She was the editor of *The Beacon Best of 2000* and *The Butterfly's Way: Voices from the Haitian Diaspora in the United States*.

Cornelius Eady, formerly director of the Poetry Center at SUNY/Stony Brook, is currently distinguished writer-in-residence at the City College of New York. He has been awarded the Academy of American Poets Lamont Prize, a Rockefeller Foundation Fellowship to Bellagio, Italy, and fellowships from the Lila Wallace–Reader's Digest Foundation and the John Simon Guggenheim Foundation.

Louise Erdrich is the author of numerous novels and books of poetry, including *Jacklight*, her first book of poems, which won the National Book Critics Circle Award. She has taught poetry in prisons and edited *The Circle*, a Boston Indian Council Newspaper. Her latest novel is *The Last Report on the Miracles at Little No Horse*. She lives in Minnesota with her daughters.

Dominican-born **Rhina P. Espaillat** writes in both English and her native Spanish. She taught high school English in New York City for several years. Her two books of poems are *Lapsing to Grace* and *Where Horizons Go*, which won the 1998 T. S. Eliot Prize. Her third book, *Rehearsing Absence*, winner of the 2001 Richard Wilbur Award, is due out in December 2001. Other awards include the Howard Nemerov Prize sponsored by *The Formalist* magazine, the "Sparrow" Sonnet Award, and three of the Poetry Society of America's yearly prizes. Espaillat directs the Powow River Poets' monthly workshop and works with Tertulia Pedro Mir, a group of Spanish-language poets in Lawrence, Massachusetts. Espaillat lives in Newburyport, Massachusetts, with her sculptor husband, Alfred Moskowitz.

John Frazier is a writer and poet living in Cambridge. His work has appeared in *Testimony: Young African Americans on Self-Discovery and Black Identity.*

Dagoberto Gilb is the author of, most recently, *Woodcuts of Women*, as well as *The Magic of Blood* and *The Last Known Residence of Mickey Acuña*, all published by Grove Press. He has been the recipient of many awards, including a Guggenheim and Whiting, and his work, besides appearing in *The New Yorker*, has been published in the *Threepenny Review, Harper's*, and the *Texas Observer.*

Francisco Goldman is the author of *The Long Night of White Chickens*, awarded the Sue Kaufman Prize for First Fiction from the American Academy of Arts and Letters, and *The Ordinary Seaman*, a finalist for the Dublin IMPAC International Literary Prize. Both novels were nominated for the PEN/Faulkner Prize. His fiction and nonfiction have appeared in *The New Yorker, Harper's, Esquire*, and many other magazines. He has received a Guggenheim Fellowship and a fellowship at the Center for Scholars and Writers at the New York Public Library.

T. E. Holt is a physician practicing in North Carolina. His short fiction has appeared in a number of literary magazines, *O. Henry Prize Stories*, and most recently in *Zoetrope*. He is working at present on a collection of essays about things that happen in hospitals, and finishing a collection of short stories about things that don't. He enjoys fishing, playing the bagpipes, and sleeping, and gets precious few chances to do any of them. He is married to a woman who works harder than he does, and has two sons who pass along advice on how to communicate with space aliens.

Ha Jin is the author of two books of poetry; two collections of stories, *Ocean of Words*, which won the PEN/Hemingway Award in 1997, and *Under the Red Flag*, which won the Flannery O'Connor Award for Short Fiction in 1996; and a novel, *In the Pond*. He lives near Atlanta, where he is a professor of English at Emory University.

Chang-rae Lee was selected as one of *The New Yorker*'s twenty best writers under forty. His work has appeared in *The Best American Essays, The New Yorker*, the *New York Times*, and numerous anthologies. The author of *Native Speaker* and *A Gesture Life*, he is the director of the MFA program at Hunter College in New York City.

Li-Young Lee's poetry has been published in the *Kenyon Review* and the *Hamline Journal*. His books of poetry include *Winged Seed, The City in Which I Love You, Rose*, and *Book of My Nights.*

Nega Mezlekia left Ethiopia in 1983. A professional engineer with degrees from Addis Ababa University, University of Wageningen, the Netherlands, University of Waterloo, and McGill University, he now lives in Toronto, where he is working on a novel.

Ishle Park is a Korean American writer born and raised in Queens. A New York Foundation of the Arts fiction grant recipient, she has been published in journals such as *New American Writing, Cream City Review, Barrow Street*, and *Manoa*. She is also one tenth of a pan-Asian spoken word collective called FeedBack and a member of the Union Square 2001 National Poetry Slam team. She currently teaches high school youth as Arts-In-Education director of the Asian American Writers' Workshop.

Pedro Ponce's work has appeared in *Alaska Quarterly Review, Ploughshares*, and *Gargoyle*.

Patrick A. Rosal, the son of Ilokano immigrants and a New Jersey native, is the author of the chapbook *Uncommon Denominators*, which won the University of South Carolina Aiken Palanquin Poetry Series Award. His poetry has appeared in *Columbia: A Journal of Literature and Art*, the *Sarah Lawrence Review, Footwork*, the *Paterson Literary Review*, and the Asian-American anthologies *The Nuyorasian Anthology* and *Streaming Monkeys*. In addition, his poems have been honored by the annual Allen Ginsberg Awards. A graduate of the Sarah Lawrence College MFA program in creative writing, he teaches literature, composition, and creative writing at Bloomfield College.

Sonia Sanchez is the author of over sixteen books, including *Shake Loose My Skin* and *Does Your House Have Lions?*, a finalist for the National Book Critics Circle Award. A recipient of numerous awards and grants, she was the Poetry Society of America's 2001 Robert Frost Medalist. She held the Laura Carnell Chair in English at Temple University and is a contributing editor to *Black Scholar* and the *Journal of African Studies*.

Danzy Senna grew up in Boston and attended Stanford University. She holds an MFA in creative writing from the University of California, Irvine, where she received several creative writing awards. She lives in New York City.

Angela Shaw was born in 1967 and grew up in West Virginia. Her poems have twice been included in *The Best American Poetry* and won a Pushcart Prize in 1999. They have also been published in *Poetry, Seneca Review, Chelsea, Field*, and *Pleiades* and have been anthologized in *The New Young American Poets*. She lives near Boston with her husband and son.

Zadie Smith is a graduate of Cambridge University. *White Teeth* is her first novel, parts of which have appeared in *Granta*. Smith lives in North London.

James Ellis Thomas is a graduate of the University of Alabama. He received an MFA from the University of Notre Dame and is currently working on a novel.

Reetika Vazirani is the author of two books of poetry, *World Hotel* and *White Elephants*. She appeared in *The Best American Poetry 2000* and received a 2000 Pushcart Prize.

Elissa Wald is the author of a collection of fiction, *Meeting the Master,* and a novel, *Holding Fire.* She lives in New York City.

Felicia Ward received the Nimrod/Hardman Award: Katherine Anne Porter Prize for Fiction in the fall of 2000. Primarily self-taught, she received invaluable training from Jewelle Gomez, in her lesbian-of-color writing groups, and at Elizabeth Stark's annual Dutch Flat Writer's Retreat. She lives in California, where she is currently a Stegner Fellow at Stanford University.

Tim Winton wrote his first novel at age nineteen and won the Miles Franklin Award for *Shallows* three years later. Since then he has published numerous books, including *The Deep* and *Blueback: A Contemporary Fable.* A passionate environmentalist, he lives with his wife and three children in Western Australia, where he grew up.

Alaska Quarterly Review is devoted to the publication of contemporary literary art with an emphasis on the works of new and emerging writers of fiction, poetry, literary nonfiction, and short plays. The *Washington Post Book World* deemed *Alaska Quarterly Review* "one of the nation's best literary magazines." Subscriptions for two double issues per year are $10 in the U.S. and $12 abroad.

Asian Pacific Journal is published semiannually by The Asian American Writers' Workshop. Each issue $10. Membership is $45 for individuals, which includes the *Journal* as well as our literary magazine, *Ten*, and discounts to our Asian American bookstore. For more information, visit www.aaww.org.

Callaloo, the premiere African-American and African Diaspora quarterly literary journal, publishes original works and critical studies of writers of color worldwide, including a rich mixture of fiction, poetry, plays, interviews, critical essays, cultural studies, and visual art. Subscribe by email: jlorder@jhupress.jhu.edu, fax: 410-516-6968, phone: 800-548-1784, or mail: Johns Hopkins University Press, Journals Publishing Division, P.O. Box 19966, Baltimore, MD 21211. The subscription options are as follows: print for individuals ($35.50); print for institutions ($86); online to institutions ($77.40); both print and online ($111.80). Postage is as follows: U.S. (free); Canada/Mexico ($9); outside North America ($18.35).

Creative Nonfiction is an internationally distributed literary journal based in Pittsburgh and edited by the award-winning author and writing professor Lee Gutkind. The first and largest journal devoted to nonfiction, *Creative Nonfiction* publishes personal essays, memoir, and literary journalism by established authors with a special emphasis on showcasing emerging talent. Each issue wraps itself around a meaningful topic, resulting in thought-provoking, high quality, accessible prose. Yearly subscriptions to *Creative Nonfiction* are $29.95 in the U.S., $35 in Canada. Visit www.creativenonfiction.org or call 412-688-0304 for more information.

DoubleTake is a magazine of documentary writing (fiction, nonfiction, poetry, and book reviews) and photography that offers new and unexpected insights about the world around us and the various ways in which ordinary people struggle to get by and get along. A one-year subscription (four issues) is $32 in the U.S.; $42 in Canada; $47 elsewhere. To subscribe call 800-964-8301, or write *DoubleTake*, Box 56070, Boulder, CO 80322-6070, or email dtmag@doubletakemagazine.org.

Gatopardo is the first Latin American monthly magazine devoted to nonfiction stories and grand reportage. Started in 2001, *Gatopardo* now has a circulation of 96,000 all over Latin America and Miami. It covers whatever is interesting to Spanish-speaking persons in Spain, the United States, and Latin America. For subscriptions ($45/year) call 888-499-1286 or write to: *Gatopardo*, P.O. Box 025720/Col 2102, Miami, FL 33102-5720.

Granta publishes new writing—fiction, personal history, reportage, and inquiring journalism—as well as documentary photography four times a year. *Granta* does not have a political or literary manifesto, but it does have a belief in the power and urgency of the story, both in fiction and nonfiction, and the story's supreme ability to describe, illuminate, and make real. Yearly subscriptions are $37 in the U.S. and the U.K.

Harper's Magazine aims to provide its readers with a window on our world, in a format that features highly personal voices. Through original journalistic devices—Harper's Index, Readings, Forum, and Annotation—and its acclaimed essays, fiction, and reporting *Harper's* informs a diverse body of readers of cultural, business, political, literary, and scientific affairs. Offering a distinctive mix of arresting facts and intelligent opinion, *Harper's Magazine* continues to encourage national discussion of topics not yet explored in mainstream media. An individual subscription in the U.S. is $21. Call 800-444-4653 or try the website (www.harpers.org).

The Literary Review is a quarterly international journal focusing on contemporary works of fiction, poetry, essays, and review essays. Subscriptions are $18 for one year in the U.S., $21 outside the U.S.

New England Review publishes a variety of general and literary nonfiction; short fiction and novellas; long and short poems; book reviews; translations; critical reassessments; statements by artists working in various media; interviews; and letters from abroad. We are committed to exploration of all forms of contemporary cultural expression in the United States and abroad. Subscription rates are $23/year (4 issues); $43/2 years (8 issues).

The New York Times Magazine is published weekly with the *New York Times* Sunday newspaper. Regional subscription rates vary. Call 800-698-4637 or visit www.nytimes.com.

The New Yorker is a weekly magazine dedicated to ideas. It is timeless and immediate, energetic and thoughtful, serious and funny. *The New Yorker* is about good writing, a point of view, and a deeper understanding of the world. To subscribe, contact *The New Yorker*, P.O. Box 56447, Boulder, CO 80322-6447, or telephone 800-825-2510 (U.S.) or 303-678-0354 (outside of the U.S.)

Nimrod International Journal is a magazine devoted to discovering emerging voices in contemporary fiction and poetry. Subscriptions are $17.50 for one year and $30 for two years in the U.S.; $19 for one year, $36 for two years outside of the U.S.

O, The Oprah Magazine is about you, your health, your spirit, your fun, and your best life. Subscriptions for a year (12 issues) are $24 in the U.S., $46 elsewhere. Visit www.oprah.com/omagazine/omag_subscribe.html, call 800-846-4020, or write P.O. Box 7831, Red Oak, IA 51591.

Poetry, founded in 1912, first published Eliot, H. D., Pound, Moore, Stevens, Williams, Sandburg, Plath, and many other classic poets. Every month, it continues to present the best in contemporary poetry. Subscriptions for 12 monthly issues are $35, available from *Poetry*, 60 W. Walton Street, Chicago, IL 60610.

Post Road is a biannual whose purpose is to publish new and emerging talent in art, criticism, fiction, nonfiction, poetry, and theater. For subscriptions ($18/year) send check to c/o Aboutface, 853 Broadway, Suite 1516, Box 210, New York, NY 10003.

Transition is a smart yet insouciant quarterly where essayists, rappers, rebel leaders, and novelists say things they won't say anywhere else. The official publication of the W. E. B. Du Bois Institute at Harvard University, it has published authors with an astonishingly broad range of views and backgrounds representing diverse disciplines. Subscriptions are available by calling Duke University Press at 888-387-5765 (U.S. and Canada) or 773-645-0982 (overseas) or visiting www.dustygroove.com/transition.htm. One-year subscriptions cost $24.99.

U.S. Latino Review is a challenging 64-page digest-sized, flat-spined literary and art journal published twice a year. It is open to all Latinos, our friends, and critics. It is dedicated to promoting the best we as a community of creative artists have to offer.

The *USLR* is a magazine published by the nonprofit Hispanic Dialogue Press. Subscriptions are $12 for one year, $22 for two years. For more information, please write P.O. Box 15009, Kew Gardens, NY 11415.

Zoetrope: All Story, published quarterly, explores the intersection of fiction and film and anticipates some of its stories becoming memorable films. Subscription rates for one year are $20 within the U.S.; $26 within Canada and Mexico; $70 for other foreign countries. *Zoetrope: All Story,* 1350 Avenue of the Americas, 24th Floor, New York, NY 10019. Fax: 212–708–0475. Website: zoetrope-stories.com.

ACKNOWLEDGMENT

Juleyka Lantigua made this anthology possible. She has been a true comrade in our community's struggle for words and una hermana without whom I could not live.

—J. D.